CHILDREN OF THE COVERED WAGON

BY MARY JANE CARR

CHRISTIAN LIBERTY PRESS

A publication of
Christian Liberty Press
502 West Euclid Avenue
Arlington Heights, IL 60004
www.christianlibertypress.com

Written by Mary Jane Carr
Revised and edited by Michael J. McHugh
Copyediting by Diane Olson
Reviewed by Sabrina Thompson
Cover Design and layout by Bob Fine
Illustrations by Bob Kuhn and Esther Brann
Clip art images on pages 21,28,69,197 and 252 are copyrighted to
Dover Publications.

ISBN 978-1-932971-50-7

Printed in the United States of America

Ad maiorem

Dei gloriam

CHRISTIAN LIBERTY PRESS
502 West Euclid Avenue
Arlington Heights, IL 60004
www.christianlibertypress.com

PREFACE

What would it have been like to leave all of the comforts of home—shelter, good food, and friendly neighbors—for the Oregon Territory in the middle of the nineteenth century? The answer to this question will become clear as you read the following story, for it chronicles the trials and tribulations of a company of pioneer men, women, and children who braved the dangers of the Oregon Trail in 1844.

Unlike many books of its kind, *Children of the Covered Wagon* provides a true and accurate picture of what pioneers heading west in a wagon train would have experienced. Readers will be drawn into the daily struggles of the pioneers as they trudged over a long and dangerous wilderness trail to reach their destination. Treacherous river crossings, scorching heat from the desert country, inhabitants of the Great Plains, and snow-capped mountains were just a few of the obstacles that routinely intruded themselves upon the weary travelers.

None but the hearty and adventurous dared to make the journey west, for disappointment and even death were common. The prospect of free land and a new start, however, caused some families to take on the risks associated with such a journey. With no guarantee that they would ever see the Oregon Territory, these brave pioneers left everything they knew, and nearly everything they owned, in the hope of a better life.

May each reader marvel at the daring exploits of the pioneers of bygone days who helped to settle the vast western wilderness territory.

Michael J. McHugh
Arlington Heights, IL
2005

Contents

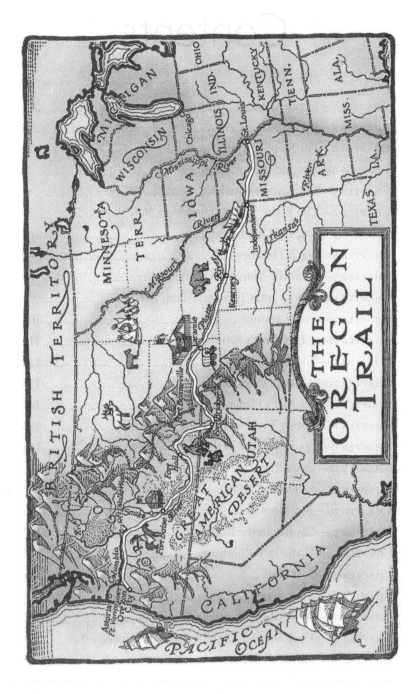

Chapter 1

Jerry and Jim

Jerry opened his eyes. It was dark, too dark for him to see anything. Someone was singing, he thought. The words of the song didn't make sense, but they had a pleasant, drowsy sound:

Creak, creak—squeak, squeak—
Thurump, thurump—creak, creak—

For a time Jerry lay listening contentedly, his mind misty with sleep. Finally he smiled. That wasn't a song at all. The branches of the big old walnut tree, brushing against the window of his bedroom, were making that squeaking, sing-song sound.

Funny! Last year—when he was ever so much younger—he used to say that the tree was scratching its fingernails on the windowpane. But how hot the room was tonight ... and how thirsty he was! He put out his hand and touched something rough and hard. The touch awakened him thoroughly. He sat up, startled—and then he remembered. He wasn't at home. He was miles and miles away from home, in a place that they called "The Prairie," and his bed was in a covered wagon. The wagon was moving. Its wheels, rolling over the bumpy ground, were making that squeaking sound that he had mistaken for a song.

A wave of loneliness swept over Jerry. He was only a little boy—just seven—and the prairie was big and filled with danger. He wasn't alone in the wagon on this dark night. His cousin, Jim, was with him; but Jim was asleep. By peering closely, Jerry could see him there in the dim light. He could touch him by reaching out his hand. Jim was going on eleven. He was a big boy, to Jerry, and he was wonderful. There was no need to be afraid of rattlesnakes, nor even Indians with tomahawks—if Jim were close. But he was asleep now, and to Jerry he seemed a thousand miles away.

There was tightness in Jerry's throat that had nothing to do with his thirstiness, and there was a hot stinging in his eyes. He was going to cry, but he remembered in time—emigrants didn't cry, and he was an emigrant—a pioneer. Jim said emigrants didn't cry. That little girl in the wagon ahead of theirs, Myra Dean, the doctor's little girl—she cried lots; but she was a girl, and a baby girl that was not even six. Jerry liked her, though. She had yellow hair that curled.

The wheels on Jim's side went down into a deep rut. Bump! Jerry had to brace himself to keep from tumbling over on Jim. Maybe that bump would wake Jim up. Jerry waited, hopefully, peering down at the sleeper. But no, Jim snuggled closer under the covers. Jerry sighed. Jim must be powerfully tired. How could he sleep through all the noise? It was strange how he could block out the creaking and groaning of big wagons, the plod-plodding of oxen hoofs, the lowing of cattle, the whinnying of horses, the barking of dogs, and the sorry cries of little calves that didn't like to be walking at night.

"Maaa! Maaa!" bawled the calves, as the shepherd dogs barked sharp, angry barks that seemed to say "stop your moaning!" There was another sound that had struck terror in Jerry's heart the first nights out on the prairie—the long, wild howl of prairie wolves. Now, after four weeks' travel, he no longer trembled at that weird voice of the wilderness; but he hated it, just the same.

Jerry coughed. His throat was so dry. The day had been hot and dusty, and they had had no water to drink since morning. That was why they were traveling at night. The men wanted to find water before they made the encampment. The cattle and horses and the big oxen that were drawing the wagons had to have water. Those poor little bawling calves were thirsty, too. Maybe they didn't understand why they were walking at night.

Sitting there in the lurching wagon, alone with his thoughts, the little boy felt a wild surge of rebellion against all this discomfort. Why did they have to go on this tiresome journey that seemed to have no end?

It was over two thousand miles! Six months it would take them, his uncle said, if they made good time.

Why did he have to leave his comfortable home—his house with its walls and roof that kept out the dust and heat and rain—his house that had a well of water right outside the door? Jerry swallowed, but the lump that filled his throat remained in place. He continued to think about his old home and his swing in the big old walnut tree ... and ice cold water! And food that was cooked on a real stove and eaten on a table with a happy red tablecloth on it, filled his mind. More than any memory, however, the dearest thought was of old Auntie Kay, who had taken such good care of him (though she was not his true aunt) that he had scarcely ever missed his mother or father. Heaven, where Auntie Kay said they lived now, had not seemed far away when he was home. Now it seemed as distant as that strange place the wagons were going to ... as far away as Oregon.

Sometimes, back home, when it was dark like this, Auntie Kay had held Jerry and rocked him to sleep. That was before he got to be seven, of course. But they had left Auntie Kay behind. She said that she had the rheumatiz and her leg joints were rusty—squeaky like the rocking chair. She was their faithful nanny, but she could never, never climb in and out of a wagon. So she remained back home in Missouri, and Jerry, who had never before been away from her, was out here, somewhere on the prairie, in a hot, jerking covered wagon, traveling toward Oregon. What did he care about Oregon? Wasn't Missouri good enough for anyone?

The words of Auntie Kay's rocking chair song came to Jerry's mind, and in a brave attempt at self-comfort, the lonely little boy started to sing, under his breath:

Honey Child, the stars are winkin'
And a-blinkin' in the sky;
Sly old sand man will come slinkin'
Round here, by and by ...

Jerry tried hard to swallow the lump in his aching throat, but it popped out with a sound alarmingly like a sob. Then there was another and another—and then there were tears on his cheeks.

"Hi, there, Jerry—you awake?" It was Jim's voice.

Jerry didn't dare turn around and let Jim see the tears. A groping hand touched his back and traveled up to his shoulder. The wagon lurched, and Jerry fell back against Jim. He stayed that way, leaning close to Jim. With a swift swipe of his fist, he wiped his wet cheeks and nose. He didn't sniff, because if he did Jim would know that he had been—well, almost crying.

"Say, isn't this great?" Jim's voice was all glad and excited. "I wish we could sleep in a moving wagon every night, us two. I'll bet Father wishes he could be riding in a wagon instead of walking out there! Wonder where we'll be in the morning! Let's look out."

Jim drew back the canvas. They looked out in silence. There was a frail new moon that gave a soft light, making everything seem lovely. Their wagon was last in line that night. It would be first in line the next day—a law of the trail. Behind them wound the cow columns, long lines of slowly-moving livestock, cattle, spare oxen, horses and mules, mounted herders riding alongside, rifles slung across their saddles. The prairie, that vast place of rolling miles, was not harsh and forbidding in this soft light. It was kind, somehow, and welcoming.

Jerry no longer felt alone. He was aware of the kinship, the nearness, of all the men and women and children in the long caravan that wound over the prairie. The cattle, oxen, mules, horses, and dogs—he felt a comradeship with them as well. He even grew to love the tired, thirsty little calves and Myra who was asleep in the wagon ahead. He would tell her, in the morning, how he had been awake at midnight ... looking out....

Creak, creak—squeak, squeak—
Thurump, thurump—creak, creak—

The funny song again ... but it wasn't a wagon-squeak this time ... it was Auntie Kay's rocking chair ... back home.... Jerry's head rolled against Jim's breast. He was asleep, comforted. Jim laid him down on the mattress and stretched out beside him. There they slept, two little pioneers. Ahead of them lay the long trail that they must travel across burning prairies and stark plains, through raging rivers, over towering mountains, among suspicious Indians and savage beasts, in drenching rain and parching heat—on to Oregon.

⁂ ‡ ⁂

The train of wagons, following the lead of scouts, finally reached water late at night—a clear, running stream. The tired men and women drank deeply, gratefully, and washed their dusty feet and faces. Then the wagons were driven into a circular position, so that the tongue of each wagon overlapped the rear of the wagon ahead, forming a barricade through which it would have been difficult for an enemy to break. The oxen were then unyoked and turned out with the other livestock to drink.

Those parched oxen and cattle and horses and mules and dogs ran to that water! Those little bawling calves that Jerry had been worrying about buried their dry noses in the cold water and sucked it up with long, noisy slurps. It was better than milk! Oh, it was better than anything else in the world! Then, after they had drunk, some of the oxen were driven into the center of the circle of wagons where they would be safe in case of a stampede, not an uncommon disaster on the trail. The cattle, horses, and mules, with the spare oxen, had been driven into the night corral and hobbled to prevent them from running or wandering away. Well-armed guards had been posted to watch over the camp, and the covered wagon travelers had rolled up in their blankets and fallen into sound sleep. The day's work was over.

❖ ┊ ❖

"Ta-ra! Ta-ra! Ta-ra!" The high, clear note of a bugle broke the quiet of morning. It was followed by the smart, ringing crack of the sentinels' rifles: Bang! Bang! Bang!

The sleepers in wagons and tents leaped up, aroused by this strange alarm clock of the trail. Another day of travel was beginning.

The dawn streaked the sky with rose and lavender. The wind brushed the prairie grass with silver. From a small grove, not far from the big encampment, came the sound of birds singing, prairie plovers and whippoorwills, the first bird songs the emigrants had heard in many days. Far off, dim and dream-like in the pearly dawn, bands of antelope flashed into view and then away.

Usually, the sentinels awakened the sleepers shortly after daybreak, as early as four o'clock, for the wagons must be on the way early, and preparation for travel took some two hours. But this morning, because of the long march of the day before, the getting-up signal wasn't sounded until five. Not all the sleepers were aroused by the call of the bugles and rifles. Jerry slept peacefully on.

"He must be powerfully tired to sleep through all that noise," thought Jim, looking down at his little cousin. "Too bad! It's a shame to wake him up," Jim said to himself, as he pulled on his trousers and shirt, "but it'd be a worse shame to let him miss breakfast."

They were going to have cornbread and molasses for breakfast—a real treat. Johnny cake, they called it. Mother had promised. She had a way of frying it in bacon drippings when there wasn't time for baking. Breakfast was never kept waiting for anyone on the trail.

Jim leaned down and called in Jerry's ear, "Hi, there, Jerry! Roll out!"

Jerry gave no sign of having heard. Jim tried another method. "Johnny cake and molasses for breakfast, Jerry!"

Jerry's eyes opened. "Hello!" he greeted Jim. "What did you say?"

Jim sniffed the air. "Smell that! Wow, it smells like johnny cake and molasses!"

Jerry sat up abruptly. "And is there water?" he asked.

"A whole river of it!" responded his taller relative.

Jerry scrambled into his trousers, wide awake now. A whole river of water, and johnny cake and molasses for breakfast. Could anything be better? The boys jumped from the wagon and made for the stream.

Now the encampment, so quiet before the call of the sentinels, was all a-bustle. Smoke was rising from dozens of fires where breakfasts were being cooked. Boys were carrying water in buckets from the stream. Shouting and laughing, they stopped, now and then, to splash one another. Girls were helping their mothers unpack pans and tin dishes. Men and dogs were rounding up the livestock. Drivers were yoking oxen. Mothers were hurrying, getting breakfasts and seeing that the little tots were dressed. There were happy morning greetings and laughter. Hardships were forgotten for the time. Everyone was excited about the birds. Spirits were high.

Jerry and Jim had been sleeping in a supply wagon behind the one they called the "Home Wagon," in which Jim's mother slept. The boys decided to head for the Home Wagon. Jerry looked with interest, as he walked, at the Deans' wagon, where little Myra slept. Myra wasn't in sight. She was still asleep—lazybones! She'd be late for her breakfast.

They found Jim's mother, a big apron tied over her calico dress, stirring something in a large bowl. She looked up at them and smiled. Her cheeks were pink from the warmth of the fire, and her dark hair, clipped close because of an attack of typhoid fever the summer before, curled about her face like a little girl's. Her eyes were very blue. Jerry often had a puzzled "remembering" feeling when he looked at her. She reminded him of someone—long ago. The little boy didn't realize that she reminded him of his own mother. In fact, she was his own mother's sister.

"Did you sleep well, boys?" she asked above her stirring.

"Fine!" answered Jim, heartily, adding, "We were awake a while last night and we looked out at the prairie. It was great in the moonlight." He said nothing about the sobs that had awakened him. "Is that johnny cake you're mixing, Mother?"

She nodded, turning to look at the skillet that sizzled on the grate above the coals and sent up the good smell of frying bacon rinds.

"Where are we now, Aunt Beth?" asked Jerry.

"Not far from the Platte Valley—the big buffalo place," his aunt answered brightly.

"Is that almost to Oregon?"

The anxious note in the child's voice didn't escape his aunt's ear. She smiled at him, but she answered soberly, "Not nearly to Oregon, Jerry—but nearer than we were yesterday morning. That is a good thing to remember, dear. Every day is nearer than yesterday."

Jerry nodded, reassured. He gave his eager attention, now, to the yellow batter that was spreading and bubbling in the hot grease. He didn't suspect that his aunt's cheery words had been spoken to reassure her own heart as well as his.

Chapter 2

Myra

Myra was awakened by a shaft of sunlight that came slanting through the opening in the back of her bedroom wagon. The place beside her on the wagon floor where her mother had slept was empty. The sun that played in Myra's blue eyes and made a halo of her yellow hair was warm, which meant that it was not an early morning sun. In fact, the hour was late, as hours were reckoned on the prairie. Nearly two hours had sped by since the sentinels had sounded the getting-up signal. Breakfasts had been eaten all along the line, and dishes had been washed and packed in readiness for the new march of the new day.

But it was not of breakfast that Myra thought first of all. It was not of her mother, even. Her eyes, losing the drowsiness of sleep, widened and darkened with alarm. She sprang up and began to search through the tumbled bedclothes. Her small fists thumped the bumps in the patchwork quilt frantically. Not there— not there. Oh, where, where? Down at the foot of the bed, she struck something hard. Holding her breath, she reached under the covers, and pulled out a doll, wrapped in a homespun shawl. She laughed aloud with relief. She kissed the doll over and over while she spoke breathlessly, "Oh, Annabelle, darling, aren't you glad it was only just a dream? Did you really think that the Indians had you and were going to scalp all your hair off?" This would have been a difficult feat for even the most practiced warrior to perform, because Annabelle's hair was only painted on her china head—a wavy black mass that could never be tangled, that never had to be combed.

Myra's imagination now pictured her terrifying dream as a thrilling adventure in which she had played a heroic part. She sang as she rocked the doll in her arms. "Don't you cry any more, honey. You're all saved now. Myra saved you."

Then, her attention captured by the sound of an angry voice outside the wagon, the little girl crawled to the opening in the canvas and thrust her tousled head out. "Hello, Michael O'Reilly!" she said.

"Heaven keep me from harm!" shouted a red-headed young man, who was tugging fiercely at a rope tied around the neck of a small but sturdy gray donkey. This agitated boy told the little beast, between tugs, just what he thought of him and the whole tribe of donkeys. The young man's face was as

red as his hair, and beads of perspiration stood out on his forehead. He let the rope fall slack in his hands and stared at Myra in surprise.

"Myra Dean, is that you? My-oh-my, I thought you were a leprechaun, poppin' out on me like that! Whatever are ye up to—not dressed yet and the whole crowd about to pull out? Come on, now, ya villain! None o' your monkey-shines!" The last portion of his comments were addressed to the donkey that had pulled back, taking advantage of the slackened rope. "Come back here, ya rogue! Thought you'd get away that time, did ya?"

"But, Michael, listen—I had to save Annabelle!"

"To save her? Whatever was she up to, now?"

"The Indians were scalping her. They had her by the hair. I screamed and screamed, but nobody came, so I had to save her all by myself!"

The little romancer sat back on her heels to observe the effect of this startling information on her audience. The young man fell into the spirit of the adventure, as Myra had known he would. Michael was as good at make-believe as she.

"Tsch! Tsch!" Michael made a sympathetic clicking sound with his tongue. "Think o' that, now! I didn't hear a single scream or I'd have come and knocked them Indians flat." He gave one last exasperated tug at the gray donkey's rope. "It's a good beatin' you're beggin' for, sirrah, and you're goin' to have it this minute." He reached for a braided rawhide whip that hung at the back of the wagon.

"Don't beat him, Michael! Let me show you!"

Myra laid Annabelle down and jumped from the wagon. Standing on bare tiptoe in the deep prairie grass, the little girl reached up to the donkey's white nose. The animal put his head down toward her hand, and she scratched his nose with her fingertips.

"Such a nice, good old fellow," Myra crooned. "Go 'long with Michael now, like a good old fellow."

"Well, I'm—a Frenchman!" exclaimed Michael O'Reilly, for the stubborn little creature that had resisted all his effort began to walk along very meekly.

"My-oh-my, it must be a gift from the Almighty you have, Myra!" the young man laughed. "I'd best be off with him now, while the influence is on him."

He started away, leading his donkey. Then he turned back, a worried frown creasing his forehead.

"That's no way for you to be, child—barefooted in the grass with rattlesnakes and all manner of varmints runnin' around." He lifted the small, nightgowned figure and placed her in the wagon. "Stay there, now, 'til I call one of the girls to get you dressed."

"Michael!" Myra called after him. "I'm going to name your donkey. I'm going to name him Beauty!"

Michael threw back his head and laughed. "I'd thought of another name for him," he said, "but if you say so, Beauty it is." He and the reformed donkey disappeared between the wagons.

Myra sat alone with Annabelle, and suddenly the happy glow went out of the morning. All around was the excitement and noise of last moment preparations for the day's travel. Men were shouting to one another as they hitched the oxen. Ox chains clanked as the big animals, frisky after the night's rest, tossed their heads, some of them trying to throw off the heavy yokes. Boys laughed and talked as they put the finishing touches of grease on the wagon hubs. No one noticed the little girl who sat with her doll in the Dean wagon. She felt forlorn and forsaken. In a few moments the long, lurching ride would begin. Myra began to cry. Where was her mother? Why hadn't she been called to breakfast with everyone else? She buried her face in Annabelle's homespun shawl and raised her voice in a wail of protest. As Jerry had observed, Myra knew how to cry. She had not yet learned the hard lesson of self-reliance the little pioneers of those stern days knew by heart before their overland journey was at an end.

"There, Myra—it's all right, little girl!"

Myra lifted her tear-stained face. Laura Thompson, a girl of nineteen, pretty as a wild rose, who taught the small children Bible stories around the campfire in the evening, climbed into the wagon. Laura and her younger brother, Dan, were orphans who were working their way west by making themselves generally useful. Everyone in the company of emigrants, including Michael, was in love with Laura. But Michael, so bold in other matters, was tongue-tied in the presence of Laura, although he and Dan were close companions.

Myra poured out her woe to Laura, in one breath, "Mother's gone and I'm all alone and I haven't had my breakfast and Michael says it's time to pull out."

"Here's your breakfast, Myra." Laura held out a bowl of steaming cornmeal porridge. "It's all sweetened and ready to eat."

Myra's eyes widened. "Am I going to eat here in the wagon when it isn't raining?"

"Yes, dear—to save time," Laura answered, getting Myra's clothing together. "Then you're to get dressed in a jiffy, and then, your mother says, you may run alongside the wagons with Jerry. You'll like that, won't you?"

"Where is Mother?"

Laura didn't answer at once. Myra looked questioningly at her and saw that Laura's eyes were red as if she, too, had been crying. Laura spoke slowly. "Your mother has been helping your father with sickness. A wagon had to drop out of line last night."

"Is the sickness better?" asked Myra.

"Better," answered Laura. Her voice quivered.

"Why were you crying, Miss Laura?"

"I was there, you know"—the girl drew a sharp breath—"and it made me sad to see the suffering. But … it's all over now. Eat your breakfast, honey."

"I'm glad it's all over," said Myra cheerfully. She scooped up her mush with hungry zest. "My father always makes sick people better, doesn't he?"

"Your father is a good doctor and a good man," said Laura, folding the bedclothes.

In the excitement of the prospect of running alongside the wagons with Jerry and Jim, Myra asked no more about the wagon that had dropped out of line the night before. Laura was thankful that the conversation ended. She didn't want to tell the child about the newly-made grave back there on the prairie. It was a tiny grave where they had buried a baby that had been born in the night and that had died before the stars had faded out.

Myra laughed suddenly. "Do you know, Michael O'Reilly said that I had a gift from the Almighty? He said that because I made his little donkey walk just by scratching his nose—the donkey's nose, I mean, Miss Laura. What do you think of that?"

Laura laughed as she tied a pink sunbonnet under Myra's chin. She kissed the glowing face on which the tears had not yet dried.

"May you always treasure God's gifts, Myra!" breathed Laura. "We need them as much as we need the ox teams to pull us through—"

"Catch up! Catch up!" The order to be on the way rang along the line of wagons, carried by hearty men's voices. Michael came running toward the Dean wagon which he was to drive that day. Laura and Myra scampered out. The day's march was beginning.

Chapter 3

The Stephen Company

It was in May, in 1844, when the green of a late spring was beginning to color the meadows and hillsides, that the Stephen Company of two hundred men, women, and children left the town of Independence, Missouri, headed for the rich valley of the Willamette River, that lay two thousand miles to the west. They had gathered at this general meeting and trading place from several states: Kentucky, Tennessee, Indiana, Illinois, Iowa, and from different towns in Missouri.

Nearly every family carried their fortunes with them in their covered wagons. The wagons were drawn by teams of oxen, sometimes three or four teams, or yokes, of the powerful animals to each wagon. Under every wagon hung a tar bucket, and a small barrel, the churn of the plains; in every wagon hung a rifle; and lashed to the tail board of many of them was a plow to be used in breaking the ground of the new land.

Where they were going there were no roads, except those made by the wheels and hoofs of previous wagon trains. With the exception of a few forts or outposts, the strange country was a vast, unbroken land, wild and treacherous. Moreover, tribes of Indians hunted the plains and mountains, fished the streams and rivers, and often warred fiercely with one another over the coveted buffalo grounds. Some of the Indians made their homes in wigwam and tepee villages, while other tribes used wood and skin lodges.

❧ ‡ ❧

The Indians, however, looked with alarm on the coming of the families from the East in their covered wagons. Small wonder that they hated the plow—to them, the symbol of a new and different way of life— that would change their hunting grounds into fields of grain, into spreading orchards and vegetable gardens. When caravan after caravan of white-topped wagons, which some of the Plains tribes called "tepees on wheels," came rolling out of the East, they carved out an indelible trail that the Indians used to call the Great Medicine Road of the Whites.

The Indians' hearts grew cold with dread, and they spoke of their fear when the chiefs of the tribes were gathered around the council fires to smoke and hold conference. "See how the whole white nation is coming in on us! The men are bringing their women and children. They are coming to stay. They are bringing a powerful medicine that we do not understand. They are killing off the buffalo, and we cannot live without them. What will become of us and our children?"

In their hearts they knew well the answer to that question. They foresaw the day, and knew it to be not many years distant, when these new settlers would have much of the land that they themselves called their own. It was a new terror. Other men in times past had come among them without disturbing their peace of mind. The trappers, who had come to hunt and to trap the sleek, small beaver, had fitted naturally into Indian life, often marrying Indian girls and making Indian ways their own. But these who came in wagons out of the East were different. They were bringing a whole new way of life with them. So the alarm of the Native Americans grew from day to day. And by the time the Stephen wagons came over the Oregon Trail, the Indian complaints that had been like the whisper of a wind sweeping through the land had grown louder and more insistent. They had become like the low rumble of thunder that warns of a brewing storm.

✦ ‡ ✦

All winter long the emigrants that made up the Stephen Company had been preparing to leave on this journey to the Far West. Getting up courage for the long trip was not the least part of their preparation. Giving up their homes, many of them comfortable homes, leaving friends and relatives, was hard to do; but the Oregon fever, once it laid hold of a man, was powerful. The lure of a golden country, where countless acres of fertile, untouched land awaited the plow, where rain fell abundantly, and where the sun never shone too fiercely, was too strong to be denied. They knew that this land could be theirs for the taking—free land!

Fathers of families talked of the West and methods of travel whenever they met. Mothers talked of it whenever two or three of them were gathered together. They talked with hushed voices and anxious glances at babies in cradles and little children playing around the doors.

"Such a hard, bitter journey!" whispered the mothers. "Too hard for delicate children. How will it end, with fierce Indians and God alone knows what dangers all along the trail?"

But they went, just the same! Their courage was stronger than their fear, and their faith greater than their doubt.

While the men got the strong wagons, which were all covered securely with canvas and painted muslin, ready, the women sorted and packed the household goods that they were to take on this long journey. Boxes and barrels and sacks of foodstuffs—flour, rice, cornmeal, sugar, coffee, tea, smoked meats, and dried fruits and vegetables—were packed. Tools of many kinds, along with firearms and ammunition, gunpow-

der, bars of lead for molding bullets, cooking utensils, iron ovens, dishes, clothing and bedding, some
books and musical instruments, herbs and medicines,
went into the wagons. Many household treasures that
would have added comfort and beauty to the homes in
the distant country had to be left behind, for wagon
space was limited, and the oxen couldn't be burdened
too heavily. But, deep in many boxes, under necessary
supplies, flower seeds and roots of shrubs and of trees
from the home garden were tucked away.

There was one little girl in the Stephen Company
who insisted, with tears, but firmly, on taking her
doll's mahogany cradle along. That little girl was Myra
Dean, daughter of the company's doctor.

"Annabelle has always slept in that cradle, ever
since she was born," Myra insisted. "How will she be
able to sleep without her very own cradle?"

Annabelle's cradle was packed in the Dean supply
wagon, and Myra danced and sang with delight; but
her mother and father looked at each other with questions in their eyes. Where would the journey end for
the heavy little cradle? Would it have to be thrown
out in some desolate place as the strength of the oxen
failed under the strain of the long, rough miles? They
wondered.

Warning had been given to families preparing for
the journey. "Leave all but real necessities here with
people who can use them," they had been advised. "It
is better to leave things behind than to have to throw
them out later to rot on the trail."

+ ‡ +

At this same time, an old nanny in Osage, Missouri, was packing the clothing of a seven-year-old boy, stopping now and then to wipe tears from her cheeks. In her heart she was crying, over and over, "I'll never see him anymore! Auntie Kay'll never see her little lamb again!"

For the child's sake, she determined to speak these words to the boy: "Jerry, aren't you glad to be adopted by your Uncle Jim and Aunt Betty, and going on such a grand ride? Way off yonder to Oregon! My! Aren't you happy, honey?"

Jerry, standing by the window and watching the road along which his uncle's wagons would come, couldn't answer Auntie Kay that he was happy. She had been everything to him since the death of his mother and father from lung fever. How could he be glad that he was leaving her? Two thousand miles was a long, long way to go from someone you loved very much. Auntie Kay was staying behind in Osage. She was too old to go on the long trail, she said.

"I'm not going forever and ever, Auntie Kay," Jerry declared, fighting with tears. "I'll come back. You just wait an' see!"

"Of course you will, honey!" Auntie Kay said it stoutly enough; but she didn't believe it. A new life and a new land would claim the child. He would forget the old nurse who had cared for him since first he opened his eyes, and who had cared for his mother before him. She would always remember, with grief, the day she parted from the young boy. This country to which Jerry was going, this Oregon, was a young person's country. Not many old people had the courage or strength to face the hardships of the trail. Auntie Kay was sixty-five.

"One, two, three, four," she counted Jerry's little shirts. She added, "Honey, don't you ever wear these best pants except to prayer meetin'!"

Tick-tock! Tick-tock! Tick-tock! The clock on the shelf was counting the moments away. To Auntie Kay it seemed to be calling: "Good-bye! Good-bye! Good-bye!"

✢ ✢ ✢

The Stephen Company of pioneers was named for Jerry's uncle, Jim Stephen, who had been elected to lead the wagon train because of his fine qualities of leadership. A lawyer by profession, he was a learned man, but he was as much at home with men as he was with books. People liked him and trusted him.

Henri Devine, a French-Canadian, and an experienced guide, was chosen to lead the way for the Stephen Company. He was a small, wiry man whose skin was bronzed out of all semblance to a white man's skin by years spent on the open trail. He knew Indians and their ways, and he knew the plains, the deserts, and mountains through which the trail westward ran.

Captain Stephen divided his company into groups or platoons of five wagons each, with a subcaptain over each platoon, who was to take care of those under his charge and report to the captain at the close of

each day. Any serious argument
or wrong con-
duct in the
company
was to
be tried
before
a judge
and jury
chosen
by the
captains.
So, banded
together, pledged
to abide by the com-
pany rules, the Stephen
Company of two hun-
dred members, with
one hundred wagons, and
nearly two thousand head of livestock—oxen,
horses, mules, and cattle—set out from Independence,
Missouri, on a May morning, in 1844, headed for the
Willamette Valley.

✦ ✛ ✦

Four weeks later, nearing the valley of the Platte
River, in what is now the state of Nebraska, then
known as the territory of the Pawnee Indians—one
of the most powerful tribes of the plains—Jim and
Jerry were happily eating their delicious johnny cake
breakfast. Myra was also busy at this point rescuing
Annabelle from the Indians.

Chapter 4

Around the Campfire

The wagons were circled in a grassy place for the night's encampment, and the boys and girls fell to work gathering wood for the supper fires. They were in high spirits, for they were going to have a big campfire that night. Michael had spotted a good-sized tree, one rare in this district, and he and Dan, taking Beauty along to help pull the tree to camp, had gone out to get it.

The children sang lustily as they gathered willow branches and scraps of wood, never forgetting, however, to stay close to camp and to keep their eyes "peeled" for danger. Emigrant children learned the use of caution early on the trail, and they liked being cautious. They liked the excitement of looking out for danger, and in the early stages of their overland travel they made games of pretending to see shapes lurking behind every likely place. At a later point, however, when Indians were a daily reality, when danger walked beside them, the game lost its charm.

When Michael and Dan came in sight, axes on their shoulders, leading Beauty, who tugged bravely at the precious tree, the children ran to meet them, shouting, "Here comes our campfire! Hurrah for Beauty!"

"Would you listen to that?" cried Michael. "Dan and I do most of the work, but it's 'Hurrah for Beauty!'"

"And it's 'Hurrah for Michael and Dan,' too!" sang out Jerry, which seemed to delight Michael, for he stood on his head and turned a series of handsprings, while the children cheered and clapped. But when Michael saw that Laura had also been watching, his face turned red and he hurried away, as if he were ashamed of his performance. Jerry thought that was curious.

After supper, men went to work with axes on the tree, and when the heavy dusk of the prairie night fell, the campfires were started. Crackling and spitting sparks, the flames went leaping high into the air. They looked like dancers, swirling and dipping, flinging veils of gray gauze about them; lovely dancers with not a care in the world. Men and women gathered, then, to sit with the children around the fires. The warmth drove them back into the fringe of darkness, and they laughed as they widened the circle.

Jerry loved the holiday spirit of the campfire hour. He was sorry for the guards who had to stay away out there in the chill dark, keeping watch over the wagons and livestock. It was good to know that they were there, keen eyes watching, rifles ready—but he was sorry for them, just the same.

Laura called her little class together—ten of the very young children, Myra and Jerry among them. Myra didn't really belong in the class, but they let her think that she did, because it pleased her. It made Jerry laugh, sometimes, when Miss Laura asked her to spell a real word, like "horse," and she answered: "C-a-t." This night, Laura was not reading Bible stories, but was coaching the children for a spelling bee. The spelling bee would only include the older boys and girls, who were gathered now, on the opposite side of the fire, with their teacher, Silas Weeks, a young schoolmaster from Kentucky.

The grown-ups tried to keep their voices low while school was in session, but now and then they forgot, and their voices rose too high. Then the teachers called the big people to order, much to the amusement of the children. And, now and again, from the inky darkness that stretched beyond the ruddy realm of firelight, came the howl of wolves—the weird voice of the prairie night. They were gathered out there, the sharp-toothed horde, at a safe distance, where they could see the camp, but couldn't be seen; where they could scent the herded livestock—a scent that tantalized them almost beyond endurance. Now and then a guard's rifle spat into the darkness as a warning to the hungry pack.

Michael O'Reilly sat on the ground near Laura's class, listening to the lesson. His eyes, when they rested on Laura, were filled with admiration. What an altogether lovely girl she was, thought Michael, entirely too beautiful and brilliant for the likes of him! That Silas Weeks, the Kentucky schoolmaster, with his polished manners and soft voice, was more to her liking, of course. Dan said she didn't care a copper about Silas Weeks—but what did Dan know about it? Michael sighed. He held a flute in his hand. When class was over and the signal for play was given, he would raise that flute to his lips, and every heart would soar with Michael's music. Sometimes he played the lilting, tender songs of Ireland, his native country; and again he broke into the bright, colorful ballads of the day that played such a truly important part in helping the pioneers across the difficult miles. The young flute player began with "Old Dan Tucker," then he played "The Girl I Left Behind." After a short break, he closed with the light-hearted refrain of "Charming Billy" and his youthful lady love:

"Oh, where have you been, Billy Boy, Billy Boy?
Where have you been, charming Billy?"
"I have been to seek a wife—
She's the joy of my life—
But she's a young thing, and cannot leave her
mother!"

Jerry liked this song best, and he sang with all the strength of his clear, treble voice:

"Can she bake a cherry pie, Billy Boy, Billy Boy?
Can she bake a cherry pie, charming Billy?"
"She can bake a cherry pie,
Quick as a cat can wink its eye—
But she's a young thing, and cannot leave her
mother!"

Other musicians joined in with their fiddles, mouth organs, harmonicas, and bugles, and the songs were taken up by the voices of the men and women and carried far out on the prairie. Here and there, a couple rose to dance, as happily as if they were treading a measure on a ballroom floor, instead of on the rough earth, far from the border of civilization.

After the evening's merriment had begun, Captain Stephen, who had been with the guards on the camp outskirts, came into the firelight. He sat down and beckoned Jim to his side. The boy came gladly. He didn't have much opportunity to be alone with his father these busy days.

"Jim," began Captain Stephen in a low voice, "some-time tomorrow we will hit the Pawnee Indian Trail."

Jim nodded, his eyes fixed on his father's face, which was very serious.

"The Pawnees are known to travelers as dangerous Indians. Devine has had news that they are inflamed with tribal war fever at this time and are in a mood for a fight. We may have no trouble with them, but we must be on our guard."

Jim watched his father's face with fascinated eyes. What had happened to change that face so? It wore an unfamiliar expression that made it seem almost like that of a stranger. The look was stern and older-looking, so much older. The twinkle that had given the eyes a boyish look was gone. Jim realized then, for the first time, the weight of care his father carried. All these people were depending on his judgment to bring them through the dangers that were beginning to hem them in. The boy's heart ached for his father.

Captain Stephen laid a hand on his small son's shoulder. "I tell you this, Jim, because I need your help," he said. "I want you to keep Jerry under your eye, all the time. See that he stays close to the Home Wagon. And do everything you can to cheer up your mother. She knows the danger we are going into. Trials like these are hard for women, Jim."

"Sure, Father! Sure I'll do that!" Jim's voice was husky.

The father looked searchingly into the sober young face turned up to his in the flickering light of the campfire. "And you won't worry, Jim?"

"Worry!" Jim was indignant. "Of course not! Only women and—and little shavers worry!"

Captain Stephen could have laughed at the scorn in the lad's voice, if it were not for the pain that gripped his heart. "Little shavers!" Jim was only ten.

※ ┊ ※

In mid-afternoon the next day, the leading wagons came upon the trail of the Pawnee Indians. The trail led from the Pawnee villages in the Platte Valley to the tribe's hunting grounds on higher levels. It was worn by years of travel. The feet of generations of Pawnees, their horses and dogs, had beaten a highway in the wilderness. In winter, these Indians kept to their villages, but with the coming of spring they roamed the prairies and plains, hunting their chief food, the buffalo, as well as deer and antelope. It was also common to see them warring over the possession of the hunting grounds with their particular rivals, the Crow and Dakota Indians.

No settler could doubt that the Pawnee was a dangerous tribe. One thing these Indians respected and admired above all others was strength. "Let the strongest take what he wants," was their motto; and it did not matter to these natives of the plains if human life was sacrificed in seizing what they wanted. Many an emigrant party, traveling in small numbers and with insufficient protection, learned this truth, to its sorrow. Horses and mules were very tempting to the Pawnee raiders. They needed them in their hunting and fighting. They took them whenever and however they could.

Blood-chilling stories of attacking Pawnees—some of them exaggerated, and some too true—had come out of this desolate country—stories that made the hearts of covered-wagon travelers faint with dread. None of them knew exactly what degree of truth was in the stories, but everyone could be certain of one thing: the Pawnees were not to be taken lightly.

Jim had watched all day for the Pawnee Trail, of which his father had spoken the night before. He hadn't told Jerry about that serious talk. Jerry was only "a little shaver." It wouldn't be right to terrify him with knowledge of the danger they might have to face so soon; but Jim kept his little cousin close beside him all day, and, with a sense of responsibility that was to grow day by day, he kept an eye on his mother, too. He did his best to keep her mind from the dark thoughts that he knew must be troubling it.

Once, when their wagons, creaking through the dust, passed a clump of blossoms, Jim gathered a handful and carried them to his mother, who sat knitting in the wagon. They weren't pretty, when one remembered the sweet-scented blooms in the gardens at home. These dust-dried flowers seemed ugly in comparison, but they were the best the barren region had to offer, and Jim's mother accepted them gladly. She buried her nose in them and that started her sneezing, but the sneezing had a good effect because it made them all laugh. They laughed until they nearly cried. Then Jim's mother fastened the bouquet at her belt and pretended with many an elegant flourish that she was dancing at a ball. Brave pretense it was, when all the time, above that little dusty bouquet, her heart was heavy with dread.

Jerry, beating time for the dance with his hands, delighted with the good humor, had no suspicion of that heavy heart, and even Jim, if his father hadn't told him of the Pawnee danger, wouldn't have dreamed of it, either. He understood now, watching his mother, that most of this grown-up confidence, that always before had been so reassuring to him, was only brave make-believe. With this understanding the boy grew suddenly older.

They had been traveling alongside the Pawnee Trail for some time before Jim knew that it was the trail he had been watching for. He learned its identity quite by accident, when one of the men rode up on horseback with a message for Dan, who was driving the Stephen Home Wagon. Jim overheard part of their conversation.

"Pretty quiet, so far," said Dan.

"Yes, but we've only hit the trail, boy! A good number of them Indians are off yonder, fightin' among themselves. Wish they'd stay there! And I'd like to have a copper for every brave that's been over that there trail!" He spurred his horse and was off in a cloud of dust.

So that was the trail. Jim looked at the well-defined highway with curious eyes. He had thought it an ordinary trail made by emigrants who had gone before them. The Pawnee Trail—what stories it could tell if it could speak! But where were the Indians?

Later in the day they came upon a rain-stained, sun-warped slab, fastened in the earth, near the trail. Jim was attracted to the spot by a group of men who had stopped to read an inscription on the marker. He bent to read the letters that had been burned into the wood. Jerry was glad of this opportunity to use his knowledge of letters on something new. He fell on his knees in the dust and started sounding the words aloud. Jim read over his shoulder:

Robert Brooks
Aged 10
Died June 1
1843

Jim drew the protesting Jerry away before he had finished his reading. A chill ran over the elder boy. This wasn't the first grave that they had passed, and their company had left a grave of its own on the prairie—that of the baby, born on the trail; but the sight of that pathetic marker of the lonely resting place of Robert Brooks, aged ten, coming as it did, after hours of nervous tension, had an almost overpowering effect on Jim. A sense of the heartache with which the dead boy's people must have gone on into the West settled like a weight on his own heart. He wanted to run away from all this sorrow and terror. But where could he run to at this stage? Oregon had never seemed so cruelly distant.

Shortly after this event, the travelers had their first sight of Pawnee Indians. Jerry and Jim stared at the dozen Native Americans who rode slowly by on horseback. They were thin and scantily clothed. They wore nothing but cinctures, or loin cloths, and moccasins. Their heads were clipped close, excepting where a ridge of bristles ran from the middle of the forehead to the crown of the head, giving them an uncanny, crested appearance. This peculiar ridge of hair was the scalp lock, an audacious challenge to enemies. They carried the short bow used by Plains Indians in shooting buffalo from horseback, and quivers of arrows were slung over their shoulders. Several of them led scrubby ponies, laden with buffalo meat. Jerry was glad to find Jim's hand grasping his own tightly.

The Pawnees rode steadily along, near enough to the wagon train to be enveloped in the dust that was stirred up by the oxen's feet and the wagon wheels; but they didn't seem to notice the frightened travelers. They rode by steadily, never altering their pace, never looking back.

Jim was puzzled by this lack of interest, but he was deeply grateful for it. He heaved a big sigh of relief. He didn't know that this indifferent manner was the pose of the clever Pawnees when contemplating mischief. In truth, not one of the wagons had escaped the scouts' eyes. They had taken note of the number of men, and of the firearms and livestock. This information would be passed on to a larger roving party of which they were members. Many fine horses were noted, sleek and of good blood! Many strong mules were seen, as well! All of these creatures would be useful to the tribe.

Chapter 5

The Pawnees Strike

Captain Stephen and Henri Devine, riding in advance of the wagon train, were the first to see the Pawnee braves. They spurred their horses forward to meet the band. Devine's knowledge of the sign language, the intertribal language of Plains Indians, made it possible for him to speak with members of all the plains tribes. He was anxious to learn something from these Indians. He hailed them with the usual verbal greeting: "How, cola!"

"How, cola!" The response that came in deep voices was cordial enough. The eyes of the mounted Indians took in every detail of the white men's equipment. They noted, with respect, the pistols and knives at their waists, and the rifles slung across their saddles, as Captain Stephen and Devine had intended that they should. The Pawnees knew well what those weapons could do. They had seen them in action and knew that they were deadly!

Devine had prepared for this meeting. He had a box of tobacco ready. The Indians accepted the luxury gladly, mumbling their satisfaction. Then Devine sought to draw some information from them. Were they members of a large hunting party? He asked. The clever raiders replied carefully. No. They had no companions. They were hunting alone. Their brothers were busy at war with bad Indians—Crows,

Dakotas—thieves that tried to take the Pawnee hunting grounds away from them. They could not stop to talk now. They must bring the buffalo meat to their hungry people. They must go far, hunting for more. They urged their ponies on and rode away. Past the wagon train they rode, watching the horses and mules with great interest.

Devine suspected that they hadn't told the truth. He advised Captain Stephen to call a halt to large campfires in this region for fear of attracting Indians to the camp. He further instructed him that it would be well to throw an extra guard about the camp that night.

So, with peril in the air, there was not much rest for the men and women after dark. Even the children, catching the contagion of fear, slept fitfully. No one knew what would befall before daylight, and, nervously, everyone feared the worst. The night, though, brought nothing unusual. The dogs barked, as they often did at night, when wolves were prowling in the neighborhood, but the guards found nothing to cause alarm. Michael and Dan took their turn at guard duty together—a duty no man of an emigrant train escaped. They went on watch at midnight. Three times Dan reported to Michael that he had seen a stealthy figure moving in the shadows. He fired and ran to the spot, but found nothing there.

"A wolf, lad," Michael suggested.

"Too large for a wolf. It was an Indian!" Dan declared.

The light of dawn was a welcome sight. Tense nerves relaxed and spirits rose with the sun. In their relief, the emigrants laughed at their fears of the night before and told jokes on one another. Michael made sport of Dan and his midnight prowler.

"Maybe 'twas a shadow you were chasin' all night, Danny!" teased Michael. "My friend, don't you know that most every shadow at night looks like an Indian? My grandfather chased one, once, in the old country, and he was a sorry man for it."

"Did he catch the shadow, Michael?" asked Jerry.

Michael's eyes twinkled, though his face was as sober as a judge's. "He did not! But he pulled the shirt off its back."

A roar of laughter went up from the listeners; but Jerry shivered with delightful chills. He loved scary stories, although remembering them at night made him hide his head under the bedclothes.

The cheer with which the morning's travel had begun failed as the hours wore on. Travel grew more and more difficult. The oxen struggled through sand hills, the sun beat down with a blinding glare, and the leaders looked in vain for water to refresh the weary travelers. Yet, that afternoon, when they came upon a grassy stretch, where a slender stream broke the sandy soil, Captain Stephen gave welcome orders to make an early encampment and turn the livestock out to graze. The country ahead was known to be rough, and the oxen were jaded and footsore. It lacked two hours of the usual night camping hour, but they could make up for the delay in the morning when they were refreshed and rested.

The wagons were driven into the customary barricade position—Captain Stephen insisted that no encampment be made without this wise precaution—and the animals were turned out. The oxen and cattle gathered in one large group; the horses and mules scattered as far as the herders would let them, hungrily pulling the short grass, wandering from one tempting tuft to another. The children tumbled and rolled like colts turned into pasture, enjoying this precious freedom from dust and heat. Some of the men began gathering wood, some busied themselves with wagon repairs, and some who hadn't slept the night before stretched out wherever they could find refuge and went to sleep, while the women worked at domestic duties around the wagons or sat and rested. A false sense of security put them off their guard. The alarm came like a thunderbolt, throwing the peaceful camp into nightmarish confusion.

"Children to the wagons! Corral the livestock! Indians! Indians!"

Devine, who had gone to the top of a sand hill to look over the country, rode furiously down toward camp, shouting the warning, "Corral! Corral!"

The children ran for the shelter of the wagon barricade. The herders leaped to hem the livestock in, to drive them to safety, but they were not quick enough. The hill was black with mounted Indians. Hundreds of Pawnees swept over the crest and down toward the camp.

Jerry and Myra, who had been playing on the outskirts of the barricade, found themselves swept along
in the mad rush of shrieking children. Jerry hadn't
seen the Indians, and he didn't try to see them. He
ran with the other children, dragging Myra along with
him. The little girl stumbled and fell, and Annabelle
slipped from her arms. Frightened as he was, Jerry
stooped and snatched the doll from under the stampeding feet. It was as important to save the doll as it
was to get Myra safely to the wagons, he thought, for if
Annabelle were lost Myra would keep them awake all
night crying for her.

Jim, not far behind Jerry and Myra, looked back
at the oncoming raiders. To his startled eyes there
seemed to be thousands of them. He thought of his
mother, alone in the wagon, and sobbed aloud, pictur-
ing her terror. But when he ran up with Jerry, he saw
with amazement that she held a glittering pistol in her
hand. Her face was pale, but calm, and she directed
the boys to stand behind her. Men were filling in the
wagon wheels with sacks and boxes to hide the movements of those behind the barricade from the Indians.
Rifles were thrust in openings, ready for action.

"Rifles ready, but no firing until ordered!" The
command given by Captain Stephen ran from wagon
to wagon. More than one man, with finger trembling
on the trigger, wondered at this command.

The Pawnees dashed down to within a few yards of
the barricade. Then, wheeling, swift as lightning, they
made for the frightened livestock. They were yelling
wildly now, and fanning the air with buffalo robes, a

certain method of causing a stampede. With the skill of much practice, they circled the horses and mules. A moment, and they were off toward the hill, driving dozens of their coveted prey before them.

Still the order held: "No firing!" Men heard it with set jaws, perspiration streaming down their faces. The Indians and the frightened horses swept over the hill and out of sight.

The oxen and cattle, stampeding in a frenzy of fear, ran in all directions. Men flung themselves on horses and made after them. It was death to the emigrants if their oxen were lost. They couldn't travel without them. Many of the women took up rifles and pistols then, as Jim's mother had done, to replace their men in defense of the camp. With weapons in unaccustomed hands that trembled, they waited, watching the hill with straining eyes. The Pawnees didn't come back. They had what they wanted. Daylight was fading when the last of the stampeded oxen and cattle were driven into camp. The men took stock of their losses then—fifty horses and mules, ten oxen, fifteen head of cattle. It was a bitter loss and one that they were to feel with increasing keenness. While they had been traveling in what they had thought was safety, the bandits of the plains had been trailing them, waiting for the moment to strike. They had judged well.

⋆ ‡ ⋆

The livestock stampede caused the first hard feelings in the ranks of the Stephen Company. Some of the men who had lost horses and cattle felt bitter toward Devine and Captain Stephen because they had not allowed them to fire on the Indians.

"The Pawnees had it all their own way," one of the men complained. "What do we carry firearms for, anyway? We had to stand by and let the Indians help themselves to our animals!"

"Likely as not, they'll follow us now, thinkin' we are afraid of them. They'll be makin' another raid seein' as how it's so profitable!" said another man.

Heads were nodded, and a murmur of agreement went around the serious-faced group.

"Listen, men," Captain Stephen pleaded, "there were at least four hundred Pawnees in that raiding party. They didn't all come down. Half of the party stayed on the hill, ready to attack if we had fired on them. Remember, they were out for horses to use in their warfare, and they were willing to take desperate measures. They didn't want scalps, but they'd have tried to take them, if we had opened fire. If we had shot one of their band, they'd have been on us like a pack of wolves. Devine knows. He's seen it happen. We have to take his guidance in cases like this."

Devine spoke up, "The Pawnees have what they wanted, and they are off now. Isn't it better that way? Aren't the lives of your wives and children worth more than your horses and mules?"

Some of the men were convinced by this argument and came up, somewhat sheepishly, to shake hands with the captain and the guide.

"Reckon you're right," said a lanky, bewhiskered Missourian, who had been loudest in his protest. "Some folks is too all-fired quick on the trigger. Come on up, you fellers! Come an' shake! Those pesky bandits didn't git all our hosses, after all."

"They didn't get my Beauty!" said Michael, trying to ease the tense feeling with a laugh. "They didn't know that they'd have to be scratchin' his nose before he'd move!"

But some of the men turned away, muttering and scowling. They went to their wagons unreconciled, and the talk spread around camp that four of the families were going to pull away and join in with a train of prairie schooners known to be a day in the rear. This grieved Captain Stephen, who had hoped to keep his company together all the way—something few, if any, captains were ever able to do. But Henri Devine took the break calmly.

"Let them weed themselves out now," he advised. "They'd be troublemakers later on, when real hardships begin. They don't know when they're well off. They've never seen an Indian massacre."

"Say, Jim, what is an Indian massacre?" Jerry asked that night. "Will we ever see one?"

"Naw!" Jim answered. "Not with Dad capt'ning this train." Jim spoke stoutly, but he felt his heart skip a beat. The thought soon entered his mind that it was high time he resume praying to the Almighty for help and protection. And moments later, Jim could be seen kneeling near a remote tree pouring out his heart to his Maker.

Chapter 6

The Platte Valley
Opens Up a New World

One morning, toiling through sand hills known as the Coast of the Platte, the Stephen Company sighted that river, the first important milestone of the trail. The emigrants stopped on an elevation and looked down on the valley in silence. The children greeted the river with cheers: "Hurrah! The Platte! The Platte!"

But the older folk were silent. Out there, beyond the river, a new world would open its doors to them— a world that was promising and yet very threatening. They would be leaving the prairies soon and entering the plains proper. Beyond the plains, the desert of cactus, alkali, poisoned water, and mirages awaited them; and beyond the desert, the Rocky Mountains, tremendous, silent, and mysterious. This was a strange and unknown country! What did it hold in store for them and these children?

Another thought, too, held them silent. Before many days they would have to cross through this river, for the trail to the mountains lay on the opposite side. Frightening stories were told of that crossing, of a strong undercurrent that swept below the seemingly shallow surface of the mighty river, a current with power to sweep huge oxen off their feet. It was also rumored that there were beds of quicksand that spread on the river floor, like traps set to snare those daring the ford.

The children knew none of these fears. They knew only that they had reached an important point in their journey and that there would be buffalo soon, and exciting new sights. So they cheered and laughed, and finally their happy enthusiasm broke the gloomy spell of silence that held their parents. The triumphant shout was taken up in older voices: "Hurrah! The Platte! The Platte!"

Men threw their hats high into the air and clapped one another on the back, talking excitedly of buffalo hunts, and of deer and antelope. Mothers laughed, with tears on their cheeks, and held little children up to see the river.

Captain Stephen looked at the Platte and the country beyond with a prayer of thanksgiving in his heart. He knew that it was the Lord's grace that had brought them to this spot. They had come now over three hundred miles since they left Missouri. They would travel along the sandy shore for a week or so before they reached the fording place. Then, on the other side, they would follow the river's course for three weeks, climbing gradually as the trail led into the ravines of the Rocky Mountains. The captain's mind leaped ahead, visioning their travel, while his company held a celebration of song and dance on the bank of the strangest river of the plains.

Jerry and Jim found it hard to get to sleep that night. The Platte seemed all that lay between them, now, and a wonderful world of adventure. They were impatient for the day of crossing. They wished it would be on the morrow. If only the oxen could travel faster! Jim fell asleep first. Jerry, wide eyes staring into the darkness, was busy thinking.

His first thought was that he would rather go around the Rocky Mountains than over them. He must ask his Uncle Jim about that option. He was boss of this trip. He might be able to change the course. Suddenly, a thrilling thought occurred to Jerry, driving out of his mind all thought of river crossings and tall mountains. Maybe he could catch a prairie dog—a puppy! He could tame it and teach it to do tricks. It could sleep in a corner of the wagon with him and Jim until it was old enough to sleep under the wagon. It would follow him everywhere. He'd let Myra play with it, once in a while, but it would be really his very own.

"Say, Jim!" Jerry's voice was an excited whisper.

A sleepy grunt came from Jim.

"Listen, Jim … you're not asleep already, are you?"

Jerry was sitting up now, peering down at Jim. Jim shivered. The night air beside the river was chilly. He opened his eyes and grabbed at the covers with a protest.

"Hey, Jerry! What're you doing, sitting up and pulling the blanket off me?"

"Say, Jim, listen! I was just thinking. Know what?"

"Why me?" Jim caught hold of the blanket and squirmed down into the warmth of the mattress, but Jerry's enthusiasm wasn't chilled.

He continued, "I'm going to catch a prairie dog, Jim, and teach him to do tricks. A puppy. He can sleep at the foot of our bed, can't he, Jim? And—"

"Please, Jerry, it's midnight! Lie down and go to sleep."

"And," Jerry went on, lying down obediently, "know what I'm going to call him? Major—or Prince, maybe. You think I can catch one, Jim?"

"Mmmmmm—" Jim was drifting back to his disturbed slumber. "Mmmm—prairie dogs aren't dogs."

"What! Not dogs?" Jerry was aghast.

"Mmmm—they're sort of … sort of rats."

"Rats, Jim?"

"Uh-huh. Rats 'r squirrels 'r something like that—" Jim's drowsy voice trailed into the deep breath of sleep.

Jerry lay for a while in silence. Then he chuckled. Jim was talking in his sleep. Funny—saying a dog was a rat or squirrel! Jerry grinned and chuckled—funny! He must think up a good name for his puppy. Would it be Major, or Prince, or Captain? So, pleasantly pondering, the little boy was carried away by sleep to dream of a puppy that stood on its hind legs and begged for a bone.

✢ ‡ ✢

The trail followed the valley of the Platte, almost due west, for more than one hundred miles before the fording place was reached. A broad valley, it was, and treeless, except where islands waved branches of willow or cottonwood. There were days when the travelers seemed to be the only living things in all the country. Once and awhile they saw traces where great beasts had rolled in the mud, and dried dung, known to plains travelers as "buffalo chips." Jerry and Jim, exploring the barren stretches with other boys, came across bones of the giant animals, bleached and polished by rain and snow and sun and wind.

One day they found an especially fine skull that Jim thought would be a good ornament to hang over the fireplace in their new home in the Willamette Valley. He and Jerry carried the skull toward the Home Wagon. They were surprised at its lightness. As they bore the treasure along, Jim made plans, "If mother doesn't want it over the fireplace, we can hang it in our bedroom. Careful there, Jerry—don't step in that sand hole."

Jerry was awed. To think that this skull was once the head of a giant animal, full of life and spirit—

the master of the plains! The big, empty eye sockets seemed to glare up at him, and in his imagination he saw the fire that once was there.

The little boy was so thrilled over carrying this relic of past power and glory that he couldn't answer Jim in words. He nodded his head vigorously to let Jim know that he realized how important it was to be careful. But, alas, their dream of carrying this trophy of the wilderness to Oregon would not last! Just as they reached the Home Wagon, where Dan trudged along beside the oxen, the skull fell apart. Jerry sent up a howl of disappointment, but Jim swallowed his dismay in silence.

"You couldn't have taken that thing west, anyway," Dan declared. "It's just as well it broke here and not in the wagon. The jolting would have smashed it. There isn't room for it in the wagon, either. Your father said at last night's meeting that we'd have to lighten our loads to get ready for the Platte crossing. Have to throw out everything but necessities. A buffalo skull isn't a necessity, and you'll soon be seeing so many of them that you'll be sick of them."

Jim let the crumbling bones fall to the ground, where they would soon become one with the sand, ground to powder beneath the marching feet of civilization.

Dan was right. Buffalo bones, skulls and all, were soon to be commonplace sights. One day, exploring near where the wagon encampment was made, the boys came across a large, cleared place where a curious design had been worked out in bleached and polished bones. Thousands and thousands of them—thigh bones, skulls, ribs, vertebrae—had been used in the intricate decoration. Half moons, stars, crosses, triangles, circles, squares, and other symbols had been arranged in a display that must have taken days of careful thought and work. Whose were the hands, and what was the purpose, behind this curious artistry?

Henri Devine explained that the display of bones was an Indian offering of thanksgiving to The Great Spirit, perhaps for some notable success in the hunting field. The little pioneers were reminded by this display that Almighty God has placed within all manner of men the need to worship their Creator. Someday, explained Henri Devine, it would be their privilege to help the Indians understand how to worship the one true God of the Bible.

About this time, the children were called on to perform a new duty, one in which they were to have much practice as the trail led farther into the buffalo country, where firewood was often not to be found for days at a stretch. The new duty was that of gathering dried buffalo chips for fuel. The chips burned with a quick, hot flame and were a perfect substitute for wood. Jim made up a game that turned the work into play. He divided the boys into teams of two, and to the team gathering the most chips in a given time, Laura presented lumps of maple sugar. Nothing they were to taste in later years was ever to have the delicious flavor of those small lumps of maple sugar won by the buffalo chip gatherers. And so, after eight days' travel in the valley, the Stephen Company reached the ford, a place several miles above a fork. At this point, the river divided to form two independent streams called the North Platte and the South Platte. The place of crossing was on the South Platte. The camp was soon buzzing with activity as the wagons were prepared for their trip through the water the following morning.

Jerry and Jim, along with all the other children, were put to work at tearing cloth into strips for use in stuffing the cracks in the wagons. In the morning, the boys would help smear the stuffed seams with tar to make them waterproof.

That night, long after the women and children were asleep, the men sat around smoldering fires, making plans for the next day's serious business. This wasn't the first river crossing they had made. The oxen and wagons had splashed through several rivers, swollen to considerable width and depth by the spring rains that were heavy that year. The Vermilions, the Big Blue, the Little Blue, and many creeks and streams had been safely forded; but none of them held the danger of this crossing. The Platte was a strangely treacherous river. A man might wade across at the ford with little trouble; but to take great, lumbering oxen and wagons loaded with supplies over the soft sand was another matter. The wheels might become mired in the sand, and if the oxen came to a standstill there was danger of their sinking hopelessly. Quicksand was a merciless captor.

They talked over methods of fording until the fires burned out. Then they sought their tents and wagons. They must be up early in the morning. The Platte lay calm and quiet in the moonlight. More than one man looked at it that night with a disquieting question in his heart: Was it mocking them, this strange yellow river of the plains?

Chapter 7

Traps of Quicksand

Several methods of crossing rivers were used by covered wagon travelers. The specific method depended upon the depth and character of the water to be crossed. Sometimes wagons were used as boats or ferries to carry the women, children, and supplies. The wheels were taken off, and all seams and cracks in the wagon boxes were calked, or filled, by stuffing them with a fibrous material or cloth. The floors were lined with buffalo robes or canvas, and then the wagon-boats were guided through the water. When the travelers were facing shallow water, oxen pulled the wagons, wheels and all, through the ford. The wagon boxes were raised out of reach of the water by blocks of wood, called "chocks," inserted under the four corners. Still another method of crossing, when timber was plentiful, was on rafts or boats, which the men made from logs.

It was decided to have the oxen draw the Stephen Company wagons through the Platte, two or three yokes of animals to each wagon, with a driver going along either side of the lead wagon to guide them and keep them moving. A test crossing was made to assure the wisdom of this plan. Dan and Michael were chosen by Captain Stephen to make the test crossing. The Stephen supply wagon was to be the first wagon through the Platte.

Lined up on the riverbank, the emigrants watched the trial crossing with anxious eyes. Down to the water went the oxen, obeying their drivers' commands.

"Gee! Haw! Steady there! Gee! Haw!"

Unlike horses, oxen needed no guiding reins. They were driven entirely by command.

"Gee! Haw! Right in, now! Gee! Haw!"

The big animals splashed out into the muddy water, finding a foothold on the slippery sand, bracing themselves against the tug of the undercurrent, drawing the wagon steadily, surely after them. The water washed up over their broad backs. Now they swam a bit; now they walked; but always they kept moving along with the patient, plodding air that marked these good beasts of burden. When the lead oxen set their hoofs on the opposite shore, cheer after cheer burst from the throats of the watchers. The ford was safe. They could follow.

"No trouble at all!" they cried to one another. "Who said this was bad traveling? Come on, let's get across."

Michael came back to tell what he had learned about the river and the sand underfoot, and the men fell silent to listen.

"There is an undercurrent, all right," he said, "but the oxen had no trouble with it. They had strength to spare. The sand is mighty soft, though, and I could feel a suction underfoot in places. The main thing is to keep the oxen moving. It would be bad if they'd stand still for even a moment."

"What's it like on the other side, Michael?" Jerry wanted to know. "Did you see the rocking mountains?"

"Nary a mountain, rocking or standing still," said Michael. "The ground is as flat as my hand. But I did see an Indian family—a man, and a woman carrying a baby on her back. They're waiting to trade with us. Maybe, now, the woman would trade her baby for Annabelle. Wouldn't that be a bargain, Myra?"

Myra had Annabelle tightly wrapped in the homespun shawl to protect her from any water that might splash up. At Michael's suggestion she shook her curly head. "No, Michael!" she answered emphatically, adding brightly, "but maybe she'd trade her baby to you for Beauty."

Michael joined in the laughter that followed this joke on him.

The crossing was soon under way. One after another, the wagons wheeled into the river, and, one after another, they came up on the opposite shore, carrying the women and children, while the men rode or walked alongside, directing the oxen. Those who had made the ford fell to work at once, gathering wood for fires, making camp, for the men would be tired and chilled by the tedious crossing and would need hot food and dry clothing. All but four of the wagons had forded the river, and men were "swimming the cattle" through, when disaster struck.

One of the lead oxen of a wagon that was over half-way across stumbled and fell, dragging his yoke mate down with him. He struggled vainly to get up. It was evident to the startled watchers that he had broken a leg. His mate managed to rise, and the drivers leaped to free him from the yoke, but the dreaded thing had been done. The wagon had been brought to a standstill. The wheels sank into the sand that had been churned to soft mud by the many wagons that had passed over it. Down to the hubs they sank, and the oxen, held by their crippled companion, struggled in terror as they felt the sand fasten like a vise about their legs. They strained in vain, heads tossing, eyes rolling wildly, trying to pull clear of the sucking sand. Their very efforts plunged them deeper. The quicksand of the Platte held them fast. Suddenly, the wagon lurched and toppled on its side. An axle-tree had broken. A voice, high and shrill with fear, rose from the sinking wagon. A woman with a baby in her arms appeared at the opening in the canvas cover.

"It's the Benjamin wagon with Mrs. Benjamin and the baby in it! They're going under! No! She's going to jump!" Sobs broke from the women. The men groaned.

Ed Benjamin held out his arms and shouted directions to his panic-stricken wife, "Throw the baby to me! I'll catch her!"

Mrs. Benjamin climbed out from under the canvas, supported herself by the bows of the tilting wagon, and, with all her strength, threw the baby toward her father's outstretched arms. He caught the little wailing bundle, passed it to other arms, and started toward the wagon. He was pulled back, roughly.

"Are you crazy, man? Look at that suction! Wait! See—they're sending help!"

Four men rode toward the sinking wagon: Captain Stephen, Henri Devine, Michael, and Dan. They dismounted, and, going as close to the sinking outfit as they dared, they spread a square of canvas out, one man holding each corner. Mrs. Benjamin stood erect, balanced herself for a breathless moment, and jumped. The force of her fall bore the canvas down into the water, all but tearing it from the hands that held it. But she was safe—she was unhurt. Laughing and crying in their relief, women on shore took the rescued mother and baby in charge. The men turned their attention to the wagon and animals, bogged in the sand.

All the supplies of the Benjamin family—their clothing, their bedding, everything they owned—were in that wagon. The doomed oxen were all that they had to carry them on the journey which had, indeed, just begun. The faces of the men were pale as they considered their predicament. They looked to Devine for help, almost as children would have looked to an older person; but Devine shook his head.

"There is nothing to be done," he said flatly, "excepting to put the oxen out of their misery. The lead yoke is drowned already. The others should be shot. Someone will have to take the family in."

"I'll take care of that," said Captain Stephen. "We'll attend to the oxen now."

He held out a hand to the owner of the mired wagon and teams. "We'll stand by you, Benjamin!"

Ed Benjamin lifted his head and squared his shoulders. "Thank you, Cap'n," he said huskily, grasping the captain's hand. "We might as well finish them now."

So they set about "finishing" the mired animals, swiftly, mercifully—the first oxen of the Stephen Company to die on the trail, but not the last!

The children, standing on the shore, heard the sharp crack of the rifle. A bright crimson spot showed in the muddy water and widened. Jerry cried silently, big tears running down his cheeks. It seemed terrible to shoot the poor animals, when they were struggling so hard to live. No one noticed Jerry's grief, for a weight had fallen on every heart. It pressed heavily and forced tears into older eyes than Jerry's.

But there was no time to give to sadness. There was work to be done. The remaining wagons and cattle were brought through, slowly, fearfully. They had to make a wide detour around the dead oxen and the wagon, of which the top alone was now visible. Campfires were burning briskly when the last wagon, dripping and glistening in the late afternoon sun, was drawn up the steep incline. The odor of cooking food was good to the travelers who had had nothing to eat since breakfast. They set themselves with determination to forget the trials of the day. "What's done is done!" became a slogan of the trail.

Chapter 8

Black Thunder

It was on the day following the Platte crossing, when the emigrants sat at their noon meal, that a warning passed through the camp: "A band of Indians is coming."

The company dogs set up a lusty barking. Questions leaped from lip to lip: Were they hostile Indians, or were they coming merely to trade? How many were there?

Captain Stephen gave word for the women and children to stay inside the wagon enclosure. The newcomers might be friendly, but there was no sense in taking chances. The captain and Devine went out to meet a band of Indians, who approached the camp on foot.

"How, cola!" said the foremost Indian, holding out his hand and grinning as if delighted at this meeting.

"How, cola!" The guide and the captain shook his hand, but drew back as the big fellow sought to embrace them.

Devine had recognized the men as belonging to the Crow tribe, unsurpassed among Plains Indians in thievery, and had warned Captain Stephen as they went out to meet their visitors, "Don't let them put their hands on you. They'll ransack your pockets."

Devine knew that stealing was considered an accomplishment by Crow Indians. They were so cunning about it that their victims often were unaware that they had been robbed until the Indians were far away. The guide had heard from Captain Bonneville, an explorer of the Rocky Mountains and Far West, an amusing account of how the Crows, once, while apparently welcoming his men into their midst with hearty embraces and evidences of great joy, had picked their pockets and deftly cut the bright metal buttons from their coats. He had often laughed at this story. He smiled, even now, as he warned Captain Stephen, "Look out for your coat buttons!"

Devine spoke in sign language with the Crow leader, who informed him, boastfully, that his name was Black Thunder. His tribe had bestowed this name on him, he explained, because of his skill in stealing horses—stampeding them by waving a buffalo robe and making a sound like that of rolling thunder. The ability to steal horses was held worthy of honor by the Crows. So Black Thunder was proud of his name.

"There are many tepees-on-wheels on the Great Medicine Road," observed Black Thunder, carefully studying the two white men.

"Many!" answered Devine. "We go across the Shining Mountains, as you know, to the land of the setting sun that lies by the Everywhere-Salt Water. There we shall build our homes and spend the rest of our days."

"Many moons will see you on the trail," said the Crow leader. "Have you food for this long travel?"

Devine recognized where this question was going. He spoke with caution. "We are prepared for long travel."

"Good! That is good and wise!" exclaimed Black Thunder. Then he shook his head mournfully. "My poor people are very hungry." With a sweep of his hand he indicated the group of men who stood behind him, well-muscled arms folded across broad chests, keen eyes watching the conversation between Black

Thunder and the white men. "Empty stomachs are bad for men. They grow faint and weak as women. They cannot hunt the buffalo. They cannot fight their enemies who come raiding their camps and driving away their best horses."

"Where are your camps?" asked Devine. He could see that the sturdy, finely-formed men before him were not suffering from undernourishment.

Black Thunder indicated that their camps were far away. The guide knew that the Crows were really far from their own district, which lay many miles to the west. But they were wide wanderers.

"Where are your horses?" Devine persisted. "Surely you didn't come that long way on foot?"

"We have few horses left," evaded the leader of the Crows. "The Blackfeet dogs! Cutthroats! They have made away with our best horses. We are very poor. White chief, give your brothers food!"

"He asks for food," Devine interpreted for Captain Stephen, "but I strongly suspect that what he wants is to get inside the wagon enclosure where his trained thieves will have a chance at our belongings. We can scrape up a meal for them, but they'll carry the news to their camp, and we'll be pestered by a whole outfit of beggars and thieves."

"But if we refuse them food, we may arouse their anger," said the captain. "Better be pestered by beggars and thieves than besieged by angry warriors. Let's try to keep their friendship. Let's feed them and let them know that one meal is all they'll get."

Devine nodded. It was the diplomatic thing to do. He turned to Black Thunder.

"Our chief says that red brothers are welcome to one meal. We can spare no more. How many are you?"

Very solemnly the Indian counted fifty, by opening and closing his upheld hands five times. Devine shook his head sternly. He corrected the count by opening and closing his upheld hands three times.

"White men know how to count, Black Thunder!" he said, looking steadily into the Indian's eyes. "Be seated, red brothers!" He indicated that they were to sit outside the wagon enclosure.

The friendly smile left Black Thunder's face. He didn't like to be told to sit outside the camp of tepees-on-wheels. Did white men treat brothers so coldly? He frowned darkly, but seeing that the white chief was unmoved by his displeasure, he sat down and signaled his followers to do the same. He spoke in a low voice to them. Devine guessed that what he said was: "Do not show anger. Those are fine knives the white men wear in their belts. They would be useful to us. We must try to get them."

Dan and several boys his age carried the coffee— "black soup" the Indians had learned to call it—and a pot of stew made of dried meat and vegetables. They also carried thirty tin cups and plates to their guests. The Indians grinned provokingly and grunted scornfully at the boys.

"White men are squaws!" they said to one another.

"The men who like to say they are our brothers are making fun of us!" muttered Dan, between clenched teeth. "I'd like to show them a thing or two!"

Inside the wagon barricade, the mothers were having a time of it, trying to keep the children quiet, for Jim and Jerry and the others wanted to be out where they could get a good look at the Indians, but the captain had ordered them to stay under cover. Who could tell how many Crows might be waiting in some nearby hidden place for a signal from Black Thunder to storm the encampment?

The Indians ate quickly. The black soup and stew were good. They wiped the plates clean with their fingers and held the empty pot out for more.

"No more!" said Devine firmly. "That is all we have cooked."

"Have you no women to cook more?" Black Thunder's face wore a sneer.

Devine's dark eyes flashed and narrowed. "We have shown friendship to you," he replied, his voice hard and cold. "We have shared our much needed food with you. We have no wish to drive you away by force, Black Thunder. Let us part friends."

For a moment Black Thunder returned the Frenchman's stare, and while the two men stood thus, regarding each other in fixed silence, the Indians in the background rose and started away. Finally, Black Thunder's eyes wavered beneath Devine's steady gaze. He turned, muttering sullenly, and followed his tribesmen. Without a backward glance, the tall, broad-shouldered figure stalked away.

"Well—they're off!" said Captain Stephen with a short laugh.

"I wonder!" said Devine. His brows were drawn in a puzzled frown. "Strange the way the others left—without waiting for a signal from Black Thunder. Seemed as if they had it all arranged—"

And so, he discovered, they had. It wasn't until the Crows were well out of reach that an embarrassing discovery was made.

"Where are the cups and plates?" one of the women asked. "We ought to give them a good scalding."

Where, indeed, were the cups and plates? Not one of them was to be found. Black Thunder and his men had carried them away.

Henri Devine and Captain Stephen grinned at each other shamefacedly. Devine would never again laugh so heartily at the way Captain Bonneville's men had allowed themselves to be tricked by the clever Crows.

➨ ✝ ➤

As the oxen strained through the sand of the North Platte shore, along which the trail now led, Captain Stephen took note of their effort. The trail now would be a gradual climb. Every wagon must lighten its load. In his mind he checked over the contents of his own supply wagon, where Mrs. Benjamin and her baby were now housed. The baby had not been well since the Platte crossing and had to be held, which meant that her mother must ride most of the time. The oxen would feel the added weight. The load must be lightened.

There was a heavy walnut chest in the wagon, an heirloom of Mrs. Stephen's family. As little Myra had pleaded to take Annabelle's cradle along, so Beth Stephen had begged to take the old walnut chest.

"Let's take it, Jim," she had pleaded, "and if it gets to be a burden—why, out it will go."

She hadn't believed it would ever get to be a burden. Captain Stephen sighed. It would be hard on Beth to give her treasure up, but the time had come. Out it must go.

※ ‡ ※

That night they made camp near the North Platte. Jerry and Jim, feeling proud of themselves for giving up their bedroom wagon to the homeless family, had been looking forward to sleeping in a tent with Dan and Michael. But just at bedtime, a terrific storm broke over the camp. Almost without warning, like some giant creature gone mad with rage, a thunderstorm swept down on the plains. It tugged at the tent ropes, pulling the pegs out of the sand, tearing at the canvas crazily. The tops of some wagons were ripped from the bows. Men and boys worked feverishly, fighting with the gale.

The wind stopped as suddenly as it had begun, and after it came a soaking, chilling rain—the bleak, disheartening rain of the open plains. The animals huddled together, heads low, backs turned to the whipping fury, the picture of dejection. Jerry and Jim scurried out of the downpour to the shelter of the Home Wagon, where they nestled gratefully under the canvas roof.

It was good to lie here, secure and warm, out of reach of the rain. They were sorry for the men who had to stay out in the storm on guard duty and for the animals that had no shelter. The dogs were huddled under the wagons, but the horses, oxen, and cattle would just have to make do. Sleep laid its quiet fingers on the tired eyelids of the boys.

Jerry was drifting pleasantly away, when a flickering light attracted his attention. Someone had lighted a taper, and there were shadows on the canvas. He heard his uncle speak. He lay drowsily watching the shadows play, paying no attention to the low-voiced conversation in the wagon, until he was aroused by a troubled note in his aunt's voice.

"But, Jim," she was saying, "to leave it here in this dreadful place! I can't bear to think of it!"

"I know, Beth." His uncle's voice was weary. "I know, but there's no help for it. We have to take the Benjamins in, and the oxen can't stand the extra burden."

They didn't speak, then, for a while. Jerry looked anxiously at his aunt. Her face was pale, and she held her lower lip beneath her teeth. Jerry was worried. Aunt Beth looked really sick. What did Uncle Jim want her to leave in this dreadful place? Finally, she spoke slowly, with a tremble in her voice.

"Of course, we must leave it, Jim," she said. "There is no other way. But I can't help hating to throw it out. It seems a part of myself. Do you remember how little Jim slept in the big lower drawer the time his cradle was burned in the fire? Remember, he loved it so that he cried for three nights after we put him in the fine new cradle you got for him?"

Uncle Jim answered with a sound that tried to be a laugh, but wasn't. "I remember how he cried, all right, but I thought it was the colic that made him cry."

"Why, Jim! The idea! Of course, it wasn't. It was because he felt that he belonged to that old chest. He felt as he would have felt in his great, great-grand-mother's arms, happy and sheltered and loved—" Her voice choked. "Oh, Jim, why are there so many hard things?"

Jerry knew now what they were talking about. It was that big, carved chest—the one Aunt Beth always kept covered with a patchwork quilt so it wouldn't get dusty and scratched. She was mighty particular about that chest. She wouldn't let him or Jim climb on it, even when it rained and they had to play in the wagon. She said it was a "dowry chest."

There was no answer from his uncle, but Aunt Beth suddenly gave a sorry little exclamation.

"Jim, dear, forgive me! As if you haven't troubles enough. I'm ashamed of myself, making all this fuss over a wooden chest ... as if it were a living thing." She laughed. "What strange notions people can get about things! Put it out the first thing in the morning, Jim, and don't let it worry you a bit."

Jerry nestled back then, reassured. It was all right. Aunt Beth didn't care so much, after all. She only thought she did, at first. But Captain Stephen understood. Still without speaking, he kissed his wife and went out into the rain to see that everything about the encampment was right for the night.

Beth Stephen tucked the covers about the boys and blew out the flickering light. She lay for a long time awake in the darkness. Her thoughts carried her far away from this rude shelter on the bank of this cruel river. Far away from these days of hardship and worry, they carried her. In fancy, she was a young girl again, in her pretty home "back East." The light of the fire, blazing on the hearth, played on the polished wood of a quaint walnut chest. Her mother, busy at the spinning wheel, was telling her the story of the chest. "And so your great-grandfather cut down the walnut tree, and after he had seasoned the wood, he made the chest, carving it, polishing it, cutting the silver hasps and bindings. A year of his spare time it took for the carving and silver-work. He wanted it to be perfect—a fit gift for his bride. Other brides in the family have owned it, and it will be yours when you marry. There is a legend that it brings joy to the owner. Happy through all her married years will be the bride who owns the dowry chest."

Beth Stephen's lips trembled in a wan smile. She had been happy, so far. But now? The dowry chest was going out of the family forever. She was not supersti-

tious, but she couldn't rid herself of a feeling of pre-
monition. A dread she couldn't explain settled about
her heart. Little Jim's first clothes were folded in the
bottom drawer, where he had slept. She must take
them out in the morning.... They were going to throw
the dowry chest away. All the tears Beth Stephen shed
over the treasure that had come, after the prideful
care of generations of brides, to lie outcast on the open
plains, were shed then in the seclusion of the wagon
and the dark.

The next morning, she took the tiny clothes from
the drawer with firm hands and a matter-of-fact manner. To Mrs. Benjamin's regretful words, she replied
lightly, "It doesn't matter, really. I should have known
better than to take it along."

Captain Stephen and Dan put the chest out beside
the trail. The ground was muddy after the heavy
rain.

"Don't you want to take this quilt off, sir?" asked
Dan.

"No," answered the captain. "Leave it as it is."

He had the strange feeling, too, that they were leaving a living thing behind.

Others of the company wagons were lightening their loads in preparation for the difficult road ahead. Here a chair, there a table, was put out beside the trail. Broken pieces of wood, warped and stained, told that others before them had done the same thing.

Beth Stephen didn't look back as they pulled away. She had asked Mrs. Benjamin to let her hold the baby for a while. The little one was restless and flushed. She held her now and sang to her as the wagons wheeled into line and pulled away. Jerry remembered for a long, long time that covered chest beside the trail. He remembered that his aunt's face was tired and pale, although she sang to the baby, and didn't seem to care about the chest. It was strange, he thought, when she had always cared for it so much.

Chapter 9

After the Monarchs of the Plains

Scouts rode ahead of the wagon train every day now, on the lookout for buffalo. The company cooks were clamoring for meat to help out the dwindling food supply, for appetites were growing sharper as the caravan climbed into higher altitudes. The little pioneers, who walked all day along the climbing trail, were hungry all of the time. Jerry thought often of Auntie Kay's red-clothed kitchen table and the good things that used to be there for him to eat. He recalled with a sort of wondering remorse that he hadn't always eaten everything Auntie Kay cooked for him. Just let him have a chance at those good things now! He was beginning to know for the first time what it was not to have quite enough to eat.

Just how much food to allow for each meal was becoming a problem for the cooks. They had to ask themselves serious questions when planning the meals. Was it wise to bake bread today? How long would that flour hold out? What would they do later, when the grass was scarce, and the cows were hungry and there was no cream to shake into butter in the small barrels under the wagons? Of course, there was the hope of replenishing their supplies at Fort Laramie—but what if supplies were low there? So many, many wagons were making demands at the fort.

And then, one evening, the happy scouts rode into camp with the news that they had located a herd of buffalo. "On the plains on the other side of the hills!" they said. "The place is alive with them!"

A thrill that burst into shouts and cheers ran through the camp. There would be fresh meat soon, and the gaunt specter of hunger would be driven far away.

The children were allowed the pleasure of sitting up late that night listening to Henri Devine's instructions to the men who were going on the big hunt on the morrow, before daybreak. The hunters' flintlock rifles, double-barreled shotguns, and pistols for close range firing were cleaned as slick as whistles. Their knives were sharpened and ready for skinning and cutting up the buffalo they felt certain of getting.

Michael let Jerry, seated on the ground beside him, hold his big shotgun across his lap, while he listened to the guide's talk. Devine, to whom buffalo hunting was an old story, had much to tell the hunters. He warned them over and over to be careful of the way they handled their weapons in the hunt. He had seen men accidentally shot by their companions in the high excitement of the chase. He cautioned them, too, that the buffalo would fight if wounded and cornered. If a man drove his horse too close to a wounded bull, the big animal would be certain to try to gore the horse with his sharp, strong horns.

"Keep your wits about you," the guide advised the listening men. "You'll need them when hunting buffalo. Pick your animals—the bulls are usually on the outskirts of the herd, guarding the cows and calves. When you shoot, aim for a vital spot—the brain, if you can, for the brain is a true mark, or the lungs; but don't think that just because a buffalo has a bullet in his hide he's done for. He is a tough beast ... none tougher, and I've known one to run for miles and then put up a good fight with a dozen bullets in him."

How great it would be, thought the younger boys, wistfully, to be big enough to hunt buffalo! This was one of the trying times when it was hard to be small.

Dan and Michael didn't sleep much the night before the hunt, and when the dawn was beginning to streak the sky, they were up and dressed, eager to be off. The hunters ate a hasty breakfast and then, mounted on the swiftest and strongest horses of the company, and taking extra horses along to help carry home the meat they hoped to get, they were off and away. In the dim, chill morning, twenty of them, young and tingling with the thrill of the hunt, rode on.

The valley was flanked by high sand hills. Beyond the hills lay a wild stretch of country known only to the buffalo, antelope, wolf, and Indian. The hunters, led by Henri Devine, headed for those hills. They soon came across unmistakable signs of their quarry. Bones lay scattered everywhere, and here and there were great dry wallows in the sands where the big beasts had rolled. Through the ravines in the hills reached deeply worn buffalo trails, where the herds came down to the river to drink. Now and then, as the light of morning deepened, the hunters saw antelope and wolves streaking through the wilderness. The wolves, slinking gray shapes, quickly bounded out of sight, but the antelope slackened their graceful pace to gaze curiously at the men and horses, strangers in their quiet world. They stood with their heads held high on slender, white throats, their lovely, dark eyes filled with wonder and interest. They let the hunters come quite close before they sped away to safety, seeming to skim through the air with incredible fleetness.

"My-oh-my, I'd have to be starved entirely before I'd shoot one of those pretty creatures!" Michael declared.

Devine laughed. "You'll be glad of the chance to shoot one before you've reached the end of the trail, my boy," he said. "But you must learn to be quiet on the hunt or you will never get the chance to shoot anything."

The guide rode to the top of a sand hill. He signaled for caution. The hearts of the hunters quickened. Their ears caught a low, rumbling sound, not unlike that of far away thunder. They followed Devine to the hilltop, dismounted, and peered down on the plains.

"Ah-h-h!" the exclamation came as one word from the lips of the men—an exclamation of astonishment and awe. Their eyes widened, and their breath quickened. There below them, so closely clustered that the plains seemed alive and slowly moving, were the buffalo, a herd of several thousand, quietly grazing, all unaware of the death that was to sweep into their midst.

Devine tossed a bit of dried grass into the air to test the wind. The buffalo's strongest sense, the one on which he depended most for warning of an enemy's approach, was his sense of smell. This sense was of little use to him as a warning if the wind were blowing in the wrong direction.

"The wind's right for us," declared Devine, as the bit of grass blew back toward the hunters. "Let's get after them."

The hunters sprang on their horses. Devine gave the signal to start, and then, bending low in his saddle to keep himself hidden as much as possible, he led the men down the hill toward the teeming plains. Finally, the outer guards of the herd sensed the presence of danger. They sniffed the air. The big bulls turned, threw up their heads, and looked in alarm at the oncoming horses. The low bellowing deepened into a great thunder of sound, and instantly the mass of animals began to move away from the approaching strangers, slowly at first, shouldering one another clumsily, and then in a frenzied rush.

Devine led the attack by lashing his horse, a trained buffalo horse, urging it directly into the herd. The other horses, new to this dangerous business, rebelled. They reared back and snorted, their eyes rolling in fright. The terror of the horses was pathetic. Quivering in every muscle, nostrils distended, foaming at the mouth, they ran to the attack, obeying the commands of their riders, and then bounded away quickly, refusing to enter the herd. The mass of buffalo broke into groups, and, as terrified as the horses, the animals made off at top speed, scattering in all directions.

When the horses discovered that the great beasts were afraid of them, that they were stampeding in an effort to get away from them, they picked up courage. The spirit of the chase entered their hearts, and away in a cloud of dust they raced, after the running buffalo.

Yelling like mad men, the hunters urged their horses on. They were beside the buffalo now, each rider trying to "spot his kill," the particular beast which he would chase and try to bring down.

Dan's mouth was dry with excitement and dust. He wasn't afraid—indeed, his heart was high with a strange joy; but his teeth were chattering, and in spite of the fact that his shirt was wet with perspiration, chills raced over him. He had spotted his buffalo, a great, heavy-humped young bull. He had run it out of the herd and was chasing it.

Foot by foot Dan's horse gained on the giant animal. The boy remembered Devine's warning to hold fire until the horse was directly alongside the buffalo, so the shot could be true. He remembered, but new to the hunt and overly anxious, he made a common mistake—he misjudged his distance and fired too soon. The shot struck the buffalo in the back. Enraged and wild with pain, the wounded giant turned on his tormenter. Head down, eyes rolling, he charged. Dan's horse leaped aside, but the buffalo was quicker than he. A sharp prong on the lunging head caught the horse's shoulder and cut to the bone. Down to his knees went the horse all a-tremble with agony, and Dan was thrown sprawling on the ground. Then, having downed his enemy

and thrown him off the trail, the buffalo turned and charged away.

Dan picked himself up after a stunned moment. He was reeling, sick and faint. His horse had struggled to his feet and stood quivering, blood streaming from the injured shoulder. The other hunters, intent on their prey, had gone on, not seeing the accident. Dan's scattered senses came back with a start when he saw the trickling blood of his horse. He knew that the animal would soon bleed to death if that flow were not stopped. The horse, a splendid young creature, was Dan's own. He had raised him from a colt and loved him as a man can love a good horse. He stood now, pain-filled eyes on his master, begging for help.

Dan tried to stop the wound with his hand, pressing the edges of the gash together with his fingers, but the crimson fluid trickled through. The ground beneath the horse's hoof was wet with blood. Looking down in desperation at the moistened earth, the boy had a thought that was like a flash of inspiration. He scooped up a handful of the wet dirt and packed it into the wound. Very thoroughly he packed it in, plastering the surrounding surface with the clay-like paste. The strange first-aid worked. Gradually, the flow was stopped. The horse's life was saved for the time, but the hunt was over for Dan.

There was nothing he could do now but stay with his wounded mount, waiting for the hunters' return, and that might be for hours. So, feeling curiously lost and weary, Dan stood and looked over the now deserted country. He could make out the figures of his companions in the distance, and those of fleeing buffalo. Here and there he saw a mound on the level ground that told him some shots had been more successful than his. Dan laughed shakily and caressed the drooping muzzle of his horse.

"You and I got ourselves into a peck o' trouble, old fellow!" he said. "It'd put a smashing end to our story if a band of Indians would sweep down on us now—"

The horse lifted his ears warningly. Dan wheeled about.

"Hullo! What's this?"

A horse was galloping toward them. Dan's heart contracted nervously. He was certain that he could make out a feathered gear on the rider's head. He gripped his rifle. But it was Michael who came riding toward him.

"I had a hunch!" Michael shouted as he slid out of the saddle. "Dan ... lad, are y' hurt?" His startled eyes were on Dan's blood-streaked face.

"Not a bit!" Dan said as he struggled to regain his composure. He felt like crying with relief at the sight of his friend. "But look here, Mike."

Michael examined the injured shoulder. He gave a long whistle. "That jab in most any other place would have finished the horse," he said. "We'll have to tear up our shirts and tie it someway. When we get him home, we'll clean it out and have Dr. Dean sew it up." Then Michael's blue eyes started to dance. "I brought a fine one down!" he cried. "We've got about ten. There'll be a feast in camp tonight!"

❖ ✝ ❖

Going over the ground to check on their game, the hunters were amazed to discover that of the ten buffalo they had shot, only three were fit for food. Seven were tough old bulls that had been roving the plains for years. Their hides, from which great patches of hair had been torn in battle, looked mangy or badly moth-eaten. There was nothing appealing to even the most ravenous appetite in the massive, dirty hulks. Devine laughed at the sight of them.

"So old they couldn't get out of your way!" he laughed. "It's a wonder the bullets didn't bounce back when they struck those hides! We'll leave them for the wolves to break their teeth on."

The guide admitted, though, that the men were fortunate to have shot three good buffalo on their first hunt, with the horses all untrained. There was as much meat on those three as they could handle, since Dan would have to ride one of the pack-horses back to camp.

The hunters learned that skinning and cutting up a buffalo was not easy for unskilled butchers. They clustered around, eager to learn, while Devine showed them the different steps. With his sharp knife, he made a slit in the skin along the backbone, after pulling the animal to its knees. Then, tugging with all his strength, he drew the skin down over each side and spread it out on the ground. As he worked, he told the men how Indian women cured buffalo skins.

They fastened the fresh skin to the ground with stakes, pulling it taut, Devine explained. Then they scraped it with knives or sharp-edged stones, gradually taking off every bit of the hair and flesh. They "flaked" it carefully, scraping off the skin that lay beneath the flesh, after which they rubbed the surface with a mixture of boiled brains and livers of the big animals, kneading the oily substance into the skin. They then folded it up, well coated with brains and liver, and let it stand for several days. After this period, they washed it thoroughly in cold water, scraped and kneaded it again, rubbed it all over with fine sandstone, and finally worked it to a wonderful softness by drawing it back and forth across a rope made of braided sinew. The hide was tied at one end to a naturally bent tree, and at the other to a stake driven into the ground.

Properly cured, Devine explained, the hide of the buffalo was as soft as cloth, and much more durable. Cured with the hair left on, the skins made warm robes, cloaks, and hats; and there were many other uses for the skin. Smoked, it was used in making moccasins and leggings. Most of the plains tepees were made from buffalo skin, although the cow was preferred for this use. The tough sinews were used by the Indian women for thread. They pierced the skin with awls or sharp stones and laced the pieces of skin together with sinews drawn through the holes.

Buffalo bones were used for making dishes, tools, and, sometimes, for arrowheads. Almost all the flesh of the animal was good, nourishing food. The tongue was considered the greatest delicacy. The fat meat of the hump was delicious, and ribs roasted over a hot fire made a dish fit for a king. The heart tasted like young beef heart, and buffalo steak was tender and juicy. From the fat, melted and freed from membrane, tallow for making candles was obtained, and, boiled with lye, the fat made good soap. There was another use for tallow, which the children of the wagon trains appreciated when they reached the alkali dust country. Tallow could be melted and smoothed over cracked and burned skin, to act as a soothing and healing ointment.

A food called "pemmican," sometimes called the bread of the plains, was made from dried buffalo meat and melted suet. The meat was pounded to a pulp with a rock, and then the pulp was put in rawhide bags, and melted suet was poured over it. To some of the bags, to provide some sweetness, sugar and berries were added. This bread of the plains, protected by the rawhide bags, would last for months and was highly nutritious. Today, this type of food is called "beef jerky."

The men cut the meat into chunks, under Devine's instructions, tied it, and slung it across the horses' backs. The scent of the flesh upset the horses. They reared back on their haunches, snorting pitifully. Poor animals! This day they were well initiated in an important part of their work of helping their masters across the continent.

As they rode back to camp, Devine warned the men to keep their eyes on the ridges of the surrounding hills.

"If you see something rise and fall, give the signal," he warned. "Those are Indian tactics. I expect some of them to be attracted this way by our shots."

The shots had, indeed, attracted the attention of a roving band, but the little party of Indians was too frightened by the powerful "sticks" that shot fire to venture close. They remained under cover until Devine's men were well away. Then they ventured down on the open plains to examine the carcasses the hunters had left behind.

It was evening when the hunters rode into camp. Anxious eyes were watching for them, and when they were sighted cheers went up from the watchers. How good the sight of the campfires was to the returning men, and the odor of cooking food that greeted their nostrils. The meat was distributed, and the delighted cooks began to work. There would be plenty of meat from now on, as they traveled in the Platte Valley, the hunters promised. Why, the place was alive with buffalo!

Dr. Dean did his first animal surgery when he sewed the gash in the shoulder of Dan's horse. Myra begged a bit of sugar to feed to the "hero horse," as she called him; but the hero horse was too sick to care about sugar, so she ate it herself.

There was a big campfire in honor of the hunters, and the children sat wide-eyed listening to the story of the chase. The little boys played at hunting buffalo, around the fire, and more than one small fellow cried out in his sleep that night, dreaming that he was being chased across the plains by a gigantic, wild-eyed beast.

Chapter 10

Rocks and Cliffs and Alkali Dust

Bump! Bump! Bump! All day long, the wagons jolted forward, for they were climbing over rough ground into the foothills of the Rockies. Jerry was afraid these days that the big prairie schooners would fall to pieces, and his fear was not unreasonable. The men were kept busy with wagon repairs, not alone because of the rough trail, but because of the increasing altitude as well. The high, dry air made the woodwork shrink and crack, and this loosened the iron bolts and wagon tires. The canvas covers that had been so dazzlingly white and clean were stained and dirty now, grizzled veterans of the trail, bearing the scars of battle with rain and storm.

Jerry knew one of his keenest disappointments on this part of the plains. It came when he saw his first prairie dog town. Until this time, he had refused to believe that prairie dogs were not really dogs. When Jim had pointed out a small, rat-like creature, now and then, telling him that it was a prairie dog, Jerry had refused to believe it.

"Wait till we come to a town of them," he told Jim. "Then you'll see that you're wrong."

But when Jerry saw his first prairie dog town, he realized without doubt that he was wrong and Jim was right. A prairie dog wasn't a dog at all.

It looked like both a rat and a squirrel. It was like a dog only in its cry that sounded like the whining bark of a puppy. It lived in a burrow in the earth. The prairie dog town to which Dan led the boys was made up of thousands of burrows, and before the entrance to each burrow sat a prairie dog, with its forepaws held up as if in prayer to the strangers not to molest it. When the boys drew near, there was a chorus of squeaking barks, and, as if warned by a leader's signal, every little animal turned a somersault and dove, head first, into its burrow.

The boys shouted and laughed—all but Jerry. He said never a word. How could Auntie Kay have made such a mistake? He must write to her and tell her the truth about prairie dogs. To make matters worse, he had promised to catch a puppy for Myra, too, and she was planning to make a bed for her puppy in Annabelle's cradle. That made Jerry feel bad. Myra would be disappointed.

Jim wanted to stay around to see whether the odd little creatures would come back out of their holes; but Jerry did not ever want to see another prairie dog. He saw many more, of course, and, as time went on, he came to enjoy the antics of the small animals. Odd little acrobats of the plains, they were, that staged a circus for the children who came in such brave numbers into their midst.

Jerry dreaded having to confess to Myra that he had been mistaken about the puppies; but Myra took the news very calmly.

"I don't care," she said. "Annabelle wouldn't have liked to have a dog in her cradle, anyway." She said that she wouldn't mind, just to be polite.

Jerry was astonished, but much relieved. Girls were funny!

And then, one morning, it seemed that the emigrants awoke to find themselves in a new world. The dreary sameness of the plains gave way suddenly to the grandeur of towering cliffs and bluffs. Great sandstone formations reared their barrier across the path so that the wagons had often to make a wide detour from the river where the bluffs forbade passage. Among the rocks the trail threaded, now winding over highlands, now finding the way back to the river through a narrow passage, where bluffs frowned down on the crawling wagons from a height of several hundred feet. They had to pass over mountains of rocks. The drivers often had to use the wheel locks now, strong chains that kept the wheels on one side from turning, to check the speed of the wagons on steep downgrades. It was the duty of the boys to take care of the wheel locks.

"Lock wheels! Lock wheels!" the drivers would cry, and the boys would jump to obey orders.

This country of rocks and bluffs was a storybook land to the children. They found it easy to imagine thrilling things as they traveled among the fantastic formations, built by the power and genius of the Creator. Here barefooted, emigrant children, dressed in faded and patched clothing, could fancy themselves romantic characters in a wonder-tale, moving through a realm of fortified towers and abandoned castles. The silent rocks were seen by the children to form a deserted city, which had been doomed to sleep for centuries. They didn't dream how near the truth their imaginings were. Someday, because they, and many like them, had passed that way in their gallant quest, this sleeping country would awake. Thriving towns and cities would, one day, rise out of the wilderness; men and women would build homes here, and children would laugh and play.

The little pioneers gave names to the towering rocks. Jim said that there were bears in the caverns of one bluff, and they named that place "Bear Cavern." Jerry thought that one rock looked like a giant asleep with his shaggy head on his arm. They named that place "Sleeping Giant." Myra insisted that one huge mass of stone was just like an angel with widespread wings. "Fluttering Angel," she called it, which caused more than one child to hope that it was a guardian angel.

Several famous landmarks of the trail were in this vicinity. Courthouse Rock, near what is now the city of Bridgeport, Nebraska, was a curiosity to the travelers—an immense domed rock of white marl that looked for all the world like an imposing building. Some claimed that it looked like the capitol building in Washington. Chimney Rock was here, and Scott's Bluff, now a national monument, gave interest to the country. Scott's Bluff was named for a gallant hunter and trapper, who, wounded and helpless, and abandoned by his companions, had died at this lonely place.

Jerry learned now that there were further disappointments on the trail. Chimney Rock was one of these. He had been looking forward to seeing a real chimney, with smoke and perhaps a few flames shooting out of it. His uncle pointed out the rock when they were over half a day's journey away from it. That was one of the marvels of this clear atmosphere. Things many miles distant often appeared only a short distance away.

"Can you see that tall shaft out there?" his uncle asked. "That is the famous Chimney Rock you've heard so much about."

Shading his eyes, Jerry peered across the miles and saw a thin black spire lifting to the sky.

"I don't see any smoke," he said. "Maybe the fire is out today."

He wondered why his uncle laughed. That afternoon he understood. Chimney Rock wasn't a chimney. It was only another rock. It was very confusing and disappointing. Why weren't things named right? But Jerry admitted that it was a wonderful rock. On the floor of the level plains it stood, a tapering shaft that rose straight as a ramrod for a distance of several hundred feet above its sturdy base of solid rock that was, itself, some three hundred feet in height.

"It looks more like a watchtower than a chimney," Jim observed. "Wouldn't it make a dandy watchtower? A person could see all over the country, if he could get to the top."

A strange country this was, and a hard one. Children who had shoes left had to wear them now, and were glad that they had saved them for the rocky trail. Others, whose shoes were gone, bound their feet with canvas and buckskin. The boys worked early and late gathering buffalo chips, an important work in this treeless country. The hunters were out from morning until night, making the most of the buffalo country that they would soon be leaving, and every wagon carried its chunks of meat hung out in the crisp air to dry.

There were constant reminders, too, of the misfortunes of other wagon travelers. Skeletons of oxen that had come to grief in the rocky region lay along the way, and the sight of deserted furniture was an everyday matter. At first the women winced and turned their eyes away from those pathetic heaps, but later they regarded them with stoic indifference. Even the graves, increasing in number from this part of the trail onward, came to be accepted as part of the price demanded by the hard country from those who sought passage through it. All unconsciously, the travelers were preparing themselves for the hardships that lay before them.

The soil began to show a film of white powder alkali dust that spoke of the desert soon to surround them. The dust filled the air when the wind blew, irritating the eyes and throats of the walkers. It sifted through the canvas and covered the wagon contents with its sharp powder. It burned the feet of the children, cracking the skin until it bled. Gone, soon, were the soft meadows of buffalo grass. Gone were the prairie dog towns where the odd little acrobats of the plains sat up at the doors of their houses. Horned toads and lizards moved among the rocks, and rattlesnakes made walking dangerous. Jerry and Jim picked cactus thorns from their toes at night. They were grateful for the buffalo tallow that soothed their parched and itching skin.

Every day brought its special trials, but the children learned not to ask their parents how much longer their journey must be. They knew that each day that went by was one day closer to their destination.

Chapter 11

Fort Laramie

The Stephen Company's first sight of Fort Laramie, longed for by all travelers of the Oregon Trail, was at noon of a blisteringly hot day. The leaders of the wagon train had climbed a hill, looked across the stream that joined the Platte and Laramie Rivers, and saw, topping a hill on the other side, a building of white clay, its bastions gleaming in the sunlight.

Far behind the bleak desert ridges that formed a background for the fort, were the Laramie Mountains, then known as the Black Hills. The mountains towered 7,000 feet high, a warning of barriers with which the wagons would soon have to contend. That didn't bother the travelers now, however. They had but one glad thought; here was Fort Laramie, at last! Here in the desert waste was a haven of rest and refreshment.

But Jerry, after his first interested look at the fort, lifted his eyes to the grim, dark hills and felt a surge of fear. They were so high! Supposing—oh it would be so easy for a wagon to slip down steep sides like those! The little boy shivered. He drew close to Jim and caught hold of his hand.

The arrival of the Stephen wagons was watched through spyglasses by Canadian employees of the fort, who perched on the rim of the high walls, like eagles, scanning the miles around. And these men were not glad to see the newcomers. Families in wagons were not new sights at Fort Laramie. They had been coming in steadily increasing numbers for the past two years, resting a while in the shadow of the fort, then wheeling on into the West. At first, the wagon caravans had been royally welcomed. But gradually, as the Indians grew resentful of their numbers, the men at the fort had come to dread the arrival of a wagon train. Not all emigrants were honest people. There were scamps and scalawags among the thousands who traveled the trail, and these bad ones stirred up trouble among the Indians. As is so often the case, innocent and God-fearing travelers had to pay dearly for the trouble other people had started.

At the time the Stephen Company drew their wagons up at Laramie, trouble was in the air. A party of emigrants had outraged the Indians recently, shooting and wounding one of their number. When the wagons had left the shelter of the fort, a band of Indian warriors had followed stealthily and attacked them. Six people, two of them women, had been killed before the vengeful attackers could be driven off.

"We'll teach the palefaces to stay at home!" the angry Indians vowed.

The natives of this region, the Oglala ("Spotted Eyes") and Brule, western bands of the Dakota or Sioux nation, were proud and haughty men. Once aroused, they were real foes. The officials of the fort were powerless to defend wagon trains after they were away from the shelter of its walls, for Laramie was not a military fort. The property of the American Fur Company, it was used solely to safeguard trade with the Indians, who came to exchange precious furs for powder, bits of colored glass, calico, and such things, trivial to most men, but very dear to the hearts of the Indians. The officials of the fort could only warn the emigrants to be on their guard, to treat the natives fairly, and to not show their fear.

The Stephen Company found a safe fording place, and, one after the other, the ox teams plunged into the river. They were not afraid of water now. They had forded so many rivers and streams that they felt as much at ease in water as they did on land. The crossing was fun for the children, who laughed and shouted as the waves splashed up, showering them with cold spray.

This wasn't like the Platte crossing. This river was clear and sparkling, for it rose in the snowy mountains, and there was no quicksand on its bed. Only pebbles were there to make a good footing for the oxen.

Jerry thought no more about dark mountains ahead, and he forgot the hardships of the trail behind them, now. Michael was singing as he guided the oxen through the water. It was good to hear Michael sing. And they could have a big campfire tonight, Jerry was sure. Very likely, too, Uncle Jim could buy lots of flour at the fort, and Aunt Beth could bake bread! Jerry took up Michael's song:

Can she bake a cherry pie, Billy Boy, Billy Boy?
Can she bake a cherry pie, charming Billy?

The world was right again. Everything was fun! The wagons wheeled to a level place, within sight of the sturdy walls of the fort, and camp was made. They planned to spend three days in this pleasant spot, laying in supplies, repairing wagons and harness, shoeing animals, cooking and washing, and resting from travel. The gloom and dread that had hung over the travelers for days was lifted now. Laughter and song came back at Laramie fort.

At the fort, where Henri Devine and Captain Stephen went at once to report the arrival of their company, Devine was greeted by a trader named Bissonette. He was a man of influence in these parts, and an old friend of his. The news that the trader gave them of Indian feeling toward the travelers was disquieting. Bissonette knew the Indians as well as he knew his own people, and Devine was certain that his friend didn't speak idly when he warned them that travel among the Native Americans of this region was dangerous. Henri Devine and Captain Stephen at once decided not to frighten the women and children with word of the danger ahead, but to hold a council of the men that night. Bissonette offered to be present at the council, an offer that was gratefully accepted.

That afternoon, when the work of making camp was over, Michael and Dan took Jerry, Jim, and Myra to visit the fort, a picturesque place always of great interest to emigrants. Michael lifted the delighted Myra to his shoulder and carried her there with many a gallop and leap. Their own laughter was drowned by the loudest chorus imaginable. This chorus was made by the shouting and talking of men and women, the yelping and barking of dogs, and the laughter and chattering of children. They paused outside the fort gate while a group of Dakota Indians, who had just crossed the river, came by carrying their whole camp equipment.

The Indians arrived on horseback and on foot, several hundred of them. Their horses and some of their dogs were laden with all that they could carry. Long poles, used to support the tepees of the camp, were fastened at one end to the horses' sides, the other end trailing the ground. Animal skins and woven willow were strapped between the poles, which formed carts in which fat, bright-eyed babies and puppies rode, amid piles of robes and utensils of all kinds. These were the travois, famous carriers of Plains Indians. The band was moving camp.

Warriors, their muscular bodies daubed with brilliant colors, arrow-filled quivers of skin at their shoulders, and bows in their hands, galloped proudly by. They were followed by their wives, who were dressed in beaded buckskin gowns, made bright with crimson paint. Their shining black hair was ornamented with embroidered bands. Horses and ponies, dripping wet from their plunge in the river, raced along. Small boys, their copper-colored bodies gleaming in the sun, darted wildly among the barking dogs.

The clatter, the color, the swift movement, bewildered Jerry and Jim; but Myra took it all as a glorious treat. Secure on Michael's broad shoulder, she clapped her small hands and waved at the racing band, laughing in delight. Her blue sunbonnet had fallen back, and her hair was a golden shimmer in the sunlight.

Suddenly, a splendid horse was pulled up in front of the little party at the fort gate. A tall Indian, powerfully built, as were most of the Dakotas, stared fixedly down at Myra. He stared as if entranced, and the child looked up at him, smiling, unafraid.

Angered by the steady stare of the Indian, Michael drew the little girl from his shoulder and held her in his arms. The Indian spoke in his native tongue, which, of course, Michael couldn't understand, but when he pointed at a group of horses, held by a young brave nearby, and then at Myra, it was clear to Michael that the man was offering to trade the horses for Myra.

"Get along with you!" Michael shouted, angrily. "You'd better be minding your own business!"

Without thinking what he did, Dan laughed at Michael's outburst. As the boy's laugh rang out, the big Indian stiffened indignantly, and the brave who held the horses rode to his side. Several others drew rein, hemming the little group in. The fort gate was opened quickly. Bissonette came out, followed by Captain Stephen and Henri Devine. The fort official spoke soothingly to the Native Americans, who listened in frowning silence. After a few moments they rode away.

"That wild man wanted to trade horses for Myra!" sputtered Michael.

"He is a powerful Dakota chief, Wolf's Brother," said Bissonette. "He thought he was honoring you by offering a trade. It's too bad you laughed. An Indian hates ridicule. Every one of those braves would have been on you in a flash if Wolf's Brother had given the word. They worship him."

"Well—he knows now that we don't want to trade, anyway," Michael said. "They have children enough of their own in that outfit without wantin' one of ours."

The incident at the gate was soon forgotten by the boys in the interest of going through the fort; but it was not forgotten by the Dakota chief, as they were to learn to their sorrow.

The image of the little girl, blue eyes laughing fearlessly, hair a crown of golden glory, stayed in the mind of Chief Wolf's Brother. "Little Daughter of the Rising Sun," he named her, and the conviction that she was a gift from the gods took hold of him. Plainly, for all the world to see, he thought, the gods had set their mark on her. Had they not taken bits of the heavens to make her eyes? Had they not wreathed her head in sunlight? Had they not given to her skin as white as the breast of the antelope? Had they not breathed into her a spirit that was fearless and friendly? Surely one so marked must have the gift of powerful medicine. Wonderful fortune would attend the camp that could call its own this radiant little maiden. Success in the hunt, the scalps of enemies, rain when the clouds withheld much-needed moisture, safety from the mighty thunder bird—these, and other gifts, would not be refused if Little Daughter of the Rising Sun asked for them! And where—the chief's heart lifted at the thought—where could be found a more desirable mate for his son who, at the age of eight summers, was already giving promise of becoming a notable chief?

Angered though he was by the laughter of the young boy at the fort gate, Chief Wolf's Brother decided as he rode toward his camp to put aside his anger and make the strangers another offer for the child. If they rejected his offer—the chief's face darkened—if they refused the honor he held out to them, he would take the child by force, and with her he would take many scalps. The scalp of the insolent one who had laughed, most assuredly, and many other scalps.

Chapter 12

Chief Wolf's Brother's Threat

Chief Wolf's Brother's village of Dakotas made camp not far from the encircled wagons of the Stephen Company. The Indians pitched their tepees of buffalo skin within sight of the emigrants, and the smoke from the supper fires of both parties mingled in the dusk of the summer evening—a peaceful, gentle scene; but the hearts of both groups were anything but cheerful that first night at Laramie.

Captain Stephen and Devine had brought the news of the recent attacks on covered wagons, and added to this anxiety was the worry caused by the chief's anger when his offer to trade horses for Myra was rejected. The captain and the guide had seen the chief's flashing eyes, and they had heard his scornful words. They also noted the gesture of one of the braves who rode up beside the indignant chief—the swift movement of the edge of his hand across his throat, the Sioux threat of revenge.

Wolf's Brother wasn't long in acting. After the evening meal, when the emigrants were gathered around campfires, the guards brought word to Captain Stephen: "A band of seven Indians is coming on horseback. All dressed up in their best beads and feathers."

Bissonette, who had come over from the fort to join in the evening's merriment, and to stay for the council of men that was to be held after the women and children were in bed, went forward with Captain Stephen to meet the Indians.

"It's Wolf's Brother!" exclaimed the Frenchman. "He's coming to make another bid for the little girl. He's really serious about it, then. You'll have to handle this thing carefully. Tell him that you are honored by his offer, and try to make him forget it. Offer gifts to him and flatter him ... but get the child out of sight."

Word was sent to the mothers to put all the children to bed at once—a chief was calling and the children might annoy him! So the little pioneers were bundled off to bed in the wagons, astonished and protesting. This was the first campfire they had had for nights and nights! Why couldn't they stay up and see the chief? They wouldn't bother him! But their protests and promises were hushed: "To bed, now! And keep very quiet, too!"

Jerry was indignant at this end of their glorious evening, and Myra cried with disappointment; but Jim knew what it was all about. His father had told him. A chief had come to bargain for Myra, and they were hiding her away from him. They were afraid! If Myra knew what the chief wanted, she would have reason to cry. Jim's heart beat double time with excitement. If only he could stay up with the men! No chief would look twice at him, with his closely-cropped hair sticking straight up on his head and his face a mass of freckles! But his father's orders had to be obeyed, so he tried to content himself with peering through the canvas and straining his ears to catch bits of the talk. There was small satisfaction in this, with Jerry leaning against his shoulder, whispering, "Look, Jim! Did you see the feathers on his head? Wow! Do you think he's an Indian giant, Jim?"

The chief was an impressive figure. Over six feet tall, broad-shouldered, slim-hipped, he moved with a graceful ease that was surprising and pleasing to see. His head was dressed in an elaborate bonnet of eagle feathers, the tails of the bonnet extending almost to the ground, and that headdress told that the chief was a brave man, for each feather in the bonnet represented a special achievement. The highest honor that could be won by a Plains Indian was that granted for touching a living enemy; for, the Indians reasoned, it required more courage to touch an enemy in battle and leave him living than to kill him. The chief wore a handsome tunic of soft deerskin, embroidered with thousands of brilliantly dyed porcupine quills. About his neck was a string of small shells, the single strand necklace peculiar to the Sioux. A wide belt of embroidered skin and moccasins that laced up the calves of his legs completed his costume. Instead of weapons, he bore a magnificent, long pipe, to indicate that his visit was one of friendship, but his shield and bow and quiver of arrows were hung at his horse's side.

Beside the chief, in the place of honor, rode a young brave, whose bare chest was marked by livid scars, proof that he was a man of almost superhuman courage and strength—one who had offered himself as a living sacrifice in the Sun Dance, the great religious rite of the Sioux. Each scar marked the place where a wooden skewer had been thrust through the flesh and torn loose after hours of tugging.

Solemn greetings were exchanged, and Captain Stephen, through Bissonette, invited the callers to sit at the campfire and smoke the pipe of friendship. What thoughts were in the pioneers' minds as they complied with this rule of Indian etiquette? Captain Stephen, Dr. Dean, Henri Devine, and the sub-captains of the wagon train all realized what the visit of the chief might mean, though not one dared to betray the emotions that surged in his heart!

When the pipe had gone the rounds, Bissonette, speaking for Captain Stephen, opened the discussion. He rose, folded his arms across his chest, and addressed the chief. "The captain is honored that the great Dakota chief, Wolf's Brother, and his brave young men have come in peace and friendship to visit this camp. The whole company will not soon forget this night."

In that last statement the Frenchman spoke the truth! Not one of them would ever forget that night, the anxiety of it, the eerie sense of disbelief that made the campfire meeting seem part of an incredible dream.

Wolf's Brother came directly to the point. As he spoke to the Frenchman, one of the braves went outside the encampment, returning in a few moments with three splendid horses, one of which had a bundle tied on its back. In silence the watchers waited while the brave untied the buckskin thongs that held the bundle in place and laid at the chief's feet a beautiful white buffalo robe and a curious object that Devine recognized as a whistle made from the wing bone of a war eagle, an article held in reverence by the Indians, who thought it to possess great power. Medicine men used the eagle wing whistle in their mystic ministrations; warriors going into battle wore it as a charm of protection; sun dancers used it in their ceremonies of thanksgiving and petition to the Great Spirit; thunder fighters, men believed to have power to frighten away impending storms, used the all-powerful whistle as part of their thunder-fighting ritual.

With an eloquent gesture, the chief pointed to the robe, the whistle, and the horses. The pioneer leaders, watching in tense silence, thought they understood the chief, even before Bissonette had interpreted his words. They thought, rightly, that he was offering these things in exchange for Myra. In reality, he was offering much more than the horses, the robe and the mystic whistle, and, at the same time, he was making a cruel threat.

Bissonette spoke slowly, carefully. "Chief Wolf's Brother says that his visit is more than a friendly call. He comes, directed by the gods, to trade with the white men."

Bissonette paused and looked at Dr. Dean. The doctor felt his heart give a bound that was painful. He knew what was coming. The interpreter continued, "Chief Wolf's Brother offers the greatest gifts in his power to give in exchange for the golden-haired child, Little Daughter of the Rising Sun, who, the Great Spirit has made known to him through his tribe's honored medicine man, Many Stars, will bring good fortune to him and to his people. He promises on his unbreakable honor to care for her as he would care for a beloved daughter, and to rear her carefully as a bride for his only son, Young War Eagle, who will be a great and powerful chief one day."

Again the Frenchman paused. Watching him intently, Captain Stephen saw a warning expression in his eyes. He continued, "Chief Wolf's Brother says that the three horses he offers are the fleetest in the land, and are trained hunters. The robe of the white buffalo is sacred. It will cover the white men from the evil spirit in their perilous journey through the mountains. The whistle made from the wing bone of the great war eagle will be a sign to all members of the Sioux nation that the men who carry it are friends who have earned the right to their protection. With these aids the journey ahead of the travelers will be safe. Without them, each mile will be fraught with great peril. Chief Wolf's Brother awaits the white chief's decision."

Then the pioneers understood! Truly this chief was well named, brother of the wolf. He was clever and cruel. In exchange for Myra he guaranteed the wagon train safe passage through Sioux territory. He would send word along the trail that the train was not to be molested. But if the emigrants refused to surrender the child, he would turn loose on them the poison of his wrath. They would be harried and hounded at every turn, and what chance would they have against the hordes the chief could turn against them?

In the silence that followed Bissonette's words, while Captain Stephen was searching his mind for just the right words—a difficult search, indeed—Dr. Dean stepped forward.

"I am the child's father," the doctor said. "I ask the right to reply to the chief."

They stood facing each other, in the leaping light of the fire, piercing black eyes meeting steady blue eyes in a look that was like the crossing of swords. Dr. Dean spoke in a calm voice. "Chief Wolf's Brother, a father, himself, will understand a father's feeling for his child. Would the chief trade his son for anything the white men could offer? Would any threat of personal harm move him to give up his Young War Eagle forever? My little daughter is only an ordinary child ... weak as all little children are weak. She does not possess supernatural power or wisdom. She would pine away, sicken and die, if she were taken from her mother and father by a strange people. We appreciate the value of the gifts the great chief offers. We know that he means to honor us—but I would not trade my child, nor allow her to be traded, for anything anyone could offer! Men do not sell their flesh and blood! Chief Wolf's Brother will understand."

While the doctor spoke, and while Bissonette interpreted his speech, the chief's expression didn't alter. He seemed busy trying to measure the spirit of this simple man who dared defy a chief. Dr. Dean returned the chief's unwavering scrutiny.

Not a man of the campfire group so much as stirred. They seemed not to breathe, so motionless they were. It was the chief's turn to speak. What would he reply to Dr. Dean? But the chief did not speak. He turned his narrowed eyes slowly from those of the doctor. He motioned to a brave, who wrapped up the buffalo robe and the eagle wing bone whistle, and bound them on the horse's back. Then, without a word, Chief Wolf's Brother and his men started away toward their horses.

Bissonette called to them. "Wolf's Brother! The captain asks you to wait. He has a gift of tobacco for you and your camp."

The chief turned his head and flashed a look of scorn at the concerned men.

"The white chief may keep his tobacco!" he said, and he and his young men rode out of the encampment.

The men sat late around the fire that night, talking in low voices. There was little they could do, other than talk. Dr. Dean had done the right thing—the only thing he could do. He had made an honest appeal to the chief's sense of justice; but the chief had apparently not responded to the appeal. In his scornful refusal of the gift of tobacco he had shown his feeling toward the pioneers. They had made a dangerous enemy.

Bissonette said that he would speak to Wolf's Brother in the morning and warn him that if the wagon train were molested, the white men's government would send an army to avenge its children; but this promise brought small hope to the men. They knew that the chief was not a fool to be frightened by empty threats. He was aware that there was no likelihood of the white men's government sending an army to avenge its children. It had not done so in the past.

A coldness, that was not so much fear as warning of trouble, settled about the hearts of the worried men. They felt themselves caught in a cruel trap from which there was no escape. They had to travel through the country of the Dakotas for many days. They must put themselves and their dear ones at the mercy of men without mercy. What chance had they? They talked until the moon was low in the sky and the stars were small and white. They laid new plans of travel, made new rules of protection, knowing all the while how weak their strongest defense would be against the powerful attack of the Dakotas.

Chapter 13

Young War Eagle

When Myra's father had appealed to the chief's love for his own child, he had touched a tender chord in the stern heart of Wolf's Brother. All the chief's strongest affection and fondest hope were centered in his eight-year-old son, Young War Eagle. As the boy had grown from a tiny fellow, the father's pride had increased.

When Wolf's Brother pictured his son's future, he saw him as a mighty chief, a power not only among the Dakotas, but one held in respect by other tribes as well; a warrior to be dreaded on the battlefield; a wise man to be looked to for weighty decisions when tribal heads were gathered for council; a leader whose name would be bright in history, and whose example would be held up before young men long after his spirit had gone to join the spirits of his fathers.

The chief took jealous care that nothing was left undone to prepare his son for this glorious future. The boy's religious and moral training and his schooling in the language and legends of his tribe had been left to his mother, White Antelope; but his physical training and his instruction in the craft of the warrior and the hunter were his father's personal care.

At eight years, the boy's well-built body was as hard as iron. Every morning of his life, Young War Eagle had

had a dip in cold water to toughen him. He had been trained to stand without flinching while his naked body was lashed with branches, to strengthen his endurance. He had learned, while still a toddler, that to cry in pain or anger, or to show fear was unworthy of a chief. He had never been sick in his life, and for all his stern rearing he was as happy-hearted as a lark. Every day, he thought, was a glorious adventure. Life was good.

When Young War Eagle had killed his first game, a bird, with his little bow and arrow, Wolf's Brother had ordered a feast prepared to celebrate the event. The camp crier, an old man whose honor it was to announce important news, went through the camp, calling the people to a feast in tribute to the chief's son. They had gathered at the appointed place—old men, who were seated in places of honor, out of respect for their age and wisdom, young men and boys, blooming young belles, withered old women, and small babies—while the glad words went round: "Young War Eagle will be a great hunter! See, already his aim is true! His hand is steady! His eyes are keen!"

Then they had seated themselves at the feast and had emptied kettle after kettle of steaming dog stew, a favorite dish among the Dakotas.

Likewise, when his son had won his first race on horseback, the chief had seen to it that the event was fittingly observed. He had called his people together and had given away several horses in recognition of the winner's horsemanship.

All this attention had not spoiled the boy, nor made him proud of himself. He accepted praise as he did punishment, in a natural, matter-of-fact manner, and all honor paid to him he laid to his father, for was it not due to his father's training, to his years of instruction and guidance, that he was able to show skill in these worthy accomplishments? Young War Eagle worshipped his father, and the chief's heart gloried in the love of his son.

So, when Dr. Dean, looking so earnestly into the chief's eyes, had asked: "Would Chief Wolf's Brother trade his son for anything the white men could offer?" the word-arrow had gone straight to its mark. The chief could make only one truthful answer to that direct question, and his sense of justice would have compelled him to agree that it was wrong to demand of another man what he would never consent to, himself, if he had not been poisoned by pride. His very love for Young War Eagle, and his fanatical ambition to provide for the boy's triumphant future, blinded the father to justice. His pride made him determined to have, at all cost, this god-given child, Little Daughter of the Rising Sun, to rear as the young chief's bride should be reared. So he closed his heart to the pioneer father's appeal. He would not answer ... in words!

The eyes of Chief Wolf's Brother smoldered as he and his braves rode toward the camp of tepees. The hearts of the young men were with their chief. They were ready to avenge his wounded pride as soon as he gave them the word. What fools these palefaces were! They were not cowards, but they were fools! The Stephen Company must be breaking camp in a few days. Soon the village of tepees on wheels would be moving into the desert, where the open miles would leave them unprotected and as helpless as small white rabbits. They had chosen this fate. The chief had promised them protection, and he had offered them the highest honor in his power to give, his own son as a mate for their daughter, but they had turned their faces away. Did they think that they could insult a chief and win forgetfulness with a gift of tobacco? They would learn better in good time.

The dark face of Wolf's Brother brightened a bit as he looked toward the camp of circled tepees. Young War Eagle would be riding out to meet him. The boy watched for his father's homecomings, and his eyes were always first to sight the tall figure of the return-ing chief. He would be riding out soon, his sturdy figure erect on his prancing pony. A frowning line appeared between the chief's dark eyes. The boy did not come—and all was not right with the camp. The uncanny intuition of the Indian made known to him the presence of disaster long before his senses gave proof of it. The fires glowed before the tepees, true, and figures could be seen moving about, but something was wrong. The heart of the chief, fearless in the wildest battle, grew afraid in the ghostlike presence of disaster that he could feel but could not see. And then his ears caught a sound that chilled his blood. It was the voice of Many Stars, the ancient medicine man. He was chanting the medicine song on behalf of someone who was in the valley of the shadow of death.

Two figures rose from the shadows and came toward the riders. One was the figure of Spirit Wind, a young mystic whom Many Stars was training to take his own place as chief medicine man of the tribe when he was dead. The other figure was that of Truth Teacher, the old camp crier. Before they could speak their news, Chief Wolf's Brother knew what it was.

Harm had come to Young War Eagle. What else than disaster to his dearest one could so weaken his heart that it grew faint as a young fawn?

"Speak!" The chief had brought his horse to a standstill and was waiting for them.

Spirit Wind spoke. "Young War Eagle was thrown from a wild horse. He is stricken by a deep sleep. Many Stars works over him now, in the medicine tepee, but, alas! His sleep is like the sleep of death."

The young man's voice held the somber cadence of the death chant.

A moment later, in the maroon-colored medicine tepee, when Chief Wolf's Brother looked down on his son, lying prostrate on a medicine robe between the fire and Many Stars's platform shrine, he saw that the sleep that held the boy was, indeed, like the sleep of death. Young War Eagle's forehead was icy to the touch, and his breath was so faint that it did not stir his chest. The racing blood had fled from his cheeks, and his skin had a strangely transparent look. His face was sharply lined by pain.

The contents of Many Stars's sacred medicine bundle were placed about the motionless figure. Medicine sticks—straight, bright-tipped rods, each holding aloft an offering to the Great Spirit—were thrust into the earth to form a guard against evil spirits around the sufferer. Scalp locks, teeth of animals, roots and herbs, whistles made from war eagles' wing bones, polished stones, each article with its own function in the medicine rite, were there. These articles, held in reverence by the tribe, often gave a false sense of hope to the Indian heart, for they represented a supernatural power over evil, sickness, and death. But sight of them held no comfort for Wolf's Brother now. Instead, a cold dread held him, for among the medicine implements laid about, he saw a human skull which he knew to be that of the medicine man who had preceded Many Stars, and who had taught him the secrets of his rites. It was the most sacred object in the medicine bundle, and was taken out only in desperate cases, and only when the life that hung in the balance was extremely precious to the tribe. Chief Wolf's Brother had seen it but once before—the night his own father's spirit passed. He recognized in it now Many Stars's admission that there was danger of the Great Spirit's refusing his petition for Young War Eagle's life. In fact, Many Stars was convinced that the little sufferer was dying.

Near the door of the tepee, White Antelope crouched, her face in her hands. She bit her lips to keep back the cry that rose to them, while around the boy's body Many Stars and Spirit Wind circled in a medicine dance, chanting vain songs to appease their god.

The mother and father watched all night, while Spirit Wind fed the fire and joined his aged master in the medicine rites. Several times the old man laid his hand on the boy's heart, expecting to find it stilled; but the strong young constitution held up. It was weakening gradually, and the medicine man, who had seen many die, knew that before the morning's sun was high in the heaven, the boy's spirit would leave his body. A changed note crept into his song of petition. He was getting ready to begin the death chant.

As the chief sat in silence, solemnly waiting for his son to be taken from him, a terrifying thought gripped his prideful mind. Perhaps the Great Spirit was taking away his son because he had tried to take away another father's child. He was so sure that he had heard from the Great Spirit that he felt justified in using threats and intimidation to try to obtain Little Daughter of the Rising Sun. Now, however, he was no longer confident that he had heard from his god at all.

The women of the camp waited near the medicine tepee, in silence. When Many Stars gave the signal, their voices would rise in a chant of grieving, the Indian song of mourning for the honored dead, that once heard was never forgotten.

Chapter 14

A Battle in the Medicine Tepee

B issonette had not slept well. All night he had tossed and turned while his mind had wrestled with the problem of how to move Chief Wolf's Brother from his determination to take little Myra. "Mais pourquoi? But why?" thought the weary Frenchman. "Why couldn't these people from the East stay at home? Weren't the States big enough for them? What more did they want? What would this resentment and bitterness that was filling the Indians' minds lead to?" These questions troubled the Frenchman as he watched the darkness pale to dawn. What a mix-up this was! He knew of another case like this—a case where a chief had taken a fancy to a white child and kidnapped him. The child had been carried into the mountains and was never seen again by his parents. That there had been other such cases he knew, for he had seen children in isolated Indian camps, whose blue eyes, blond hair, and Caucasian features told plainly that no Indian blood ran in their veins.

When daylight came, Bissonette arose, determined to make a supreme effort to turn the stubborn chief from his dark purpose. As he rode toward the Dakota camp, he formed a plan. He would make his appeal to Wolf's Brother in the form of a threat, working on the native Indian superstition. He would tell the chief that the little girl was the only child of a great white medicine man who could bring death and destruction on the tribe that dared to steal his most precious possession. As his foolish plan took shape, Bissonette's hope soared, but it was dashed by the news that met him at the Dakota camp. Young War Eagle's injury lent new gravity to the problem. If the boy died, the Indians may well lay the disaster to some evil power invoked by the white men. It might lead to a massacre. Bissonette groaned in despair as he turned back toward Fort Laramie. What was to be done now?

Suddenly, a thought that had the power of inspiration leaped into his mind. There might be a chance, even now! It would be a desperate chance, but this whole situation was desperate. He turned his horse toward the wagon camp and rode at top speed. When he rode back, a short time later, Dr. Dean rode with him. The doctor's face was pale and grim. He had the strained look of a man going into battle from which there might be no returning.

Bissonette explained, as they rode side by side, frequently lapsing into his native French in his haste and excitement, "If you can save him, everything may be won. If you fail—well, things can't be much worse than they are now. The boy is dying, they say, but it may be that Many Stars is mistaken. Maybe he hasn't tried any natural remedies. He was a powerful medicine man in his day, but he is old now, and failing fast. He is nearly a spirit, himself, and he thinks only in terms of the spirit. Chief Wolf's Brother knows me and will listen to me, at any rate. I'll try to convince him that you can cure the boy."

Dr. Dean didn't speak. His thoughts raced ahead of their horses to the tepee where the chief's son lay close to death. The boy had been thrown from a wild horse, likely striking on his head. He had lain all night in a stupor. Perhaps the skull was fractured. Even if the chief did give him permission to try, would it be possible to save the boy after that long neglect?

What chance did he have, after all? He was regarded as one of the invaders of Native American lands. He was mistrusted and hated by the Dakota people. Now he would be working directly against the medicine man, who was revered and idolized by the tribe! His medical skill, with all the odds against it, was pitted against their age-old beliefs, the origin of which no man knew. But no!—the thought came with the comfort of firmly spoken words. He was not relying on his medical skill alone. His Christian faith, his trust in the grace and mercy of Almighty God, would come to his assistance now. God alone would give him the courage he needed to help another human being. At once, strength and calmness came to Dr. Dean. He lost all feelings of fear and doom, and he knew only a great eagerness to do all he could to save the young life that was ebbing away, if God willed.

When the two men drew near the medicine tepee, they found that the boy had been carried outside in accordance with the Indian belief that one should die under the roof of heaven, the open sky. Young War Eagle lay on a white buffalo robe. His mother was prostrate on the earth nearby. When her son breathed his last, she would slash her own flesh in the abandonment of her grief. Indian women often cut off their fingertips or otherwise maimed and disfigured themselves when someone they loved left the world. Chief Wolf's Brother was meeting his sorrow standing, as befitted a man and a chief.

Dr. Dean's eyes sought the boy's face anxiously. He still lived. The doctor clenched his teeth and dug his fingernails into his palms in his anxiety to get to work—to shield that flickering flame of life. Every second was vital. Standing there, looking down at the child, he was already at work, planning each move he would make, if the chief gave permission—if only he would let him try to save his son.

Bissonette stepped to Wolf's Brother's side and spoke earnestly. The chief looked at him dully, at first, seeming not to know nor care what he was talking about. But suddenly, he wheeled and faced Dr. Dean. Something fierce and stirring leaped into the dark eyes. It was evident that Bissonette had judged correctly. Wolf's Brother already associated this misfortune that had befallen him with the unwelcome strangers.

Dr. Dean met the chief's eyes fairly. Sometimes the spirit speaks more clearly than the tongue and speaks a language any man can understand. The doctor had forgotten all fear of personal danger in his pity for this afflicted father, and his sincerity, his desire to help, showed in his eyes and spoke to the chief's heart. The fierce eyes softened, and a look of appeal filled them. Wolf's Brother turned to Bissonette and listened carefully.

"The white medicine man has come to help you, Chief Wolf's Brother!" Bissonette was saying. "He has a powerful medicine. It has called back many as near the threshold of death as is your son. Let him try his medicine, Wolf's Brother! Young War Eagle should live many more years. He should be a powerful chief. Let the white medicine man work with Many Stars. Are not two more powerful than one?"

The chief looked questioningly at Many Stars. He was torn between the desire to try the white man's medicine and the fear of going against the wishes of his tribe's honored wise man.

The Frenchman addressed his appeal to the aged medicine man. "Many Stars, wise one! You prayed and, lo, the gods have answered your prayer! See, they have sent this white medicine man with a wonderful new medicine! He will teach you how to use it, and your people will honor you more than they have yet honored you! Do you consent, Many Stars?"

White Antelope, who had risen to her knees as Bissonette spoke, rose now from the ground and held out her arms in supplication. "Oh, Many Stars, consent!" she implored. "Take this help the gods have sent to you!"

The old man considered for a moment. If he refused to let the medicine man work with him, the people would murmur, displeased. The boy was marked for death. Nothing could save him now. Sometimes, when one as dearly loved as Young War Eagle died, the tribe turned against the medicine man and killed him. It would be wise to have this white man to blame when the youth's spirit passed. Then the people could vent their grief on him. Let the white man try—and fail! Many Stars made a submissive gesture. The chief stepped back. The way was clear for Dr. Dean.

The doctor was at work on Young War Eagle instantly. His hands went searchingly over the boy's head. He lifted the closed lids and peered into the dull eyes. He took note of pulse and breathing, and he was satisfied that there was no fracture. The boy suffered from a severe concussion, he decided. If he had been properly cared for at first, he would have responded well; but now—well, he was still alive, and that was all. He carried his patient back into the medicine tepee and laid him near the smoldering fire. While he administered a powerful stimulant, the fire was built up and rocks were heated to pack around the chilled body. The doctor noted with joy that the reaction to the stimulant was good. The fluttering heart beat stronger, and the blood that had so nearly congealed started circulating more freely. The heat from the rocks gave warmth to the chilled body. The fight against death had begun. It would be a hard one.

At times, it seemed to Dr. Dean that it was not this Indian child he fought to save, but his own little Myra, and, as he worked, he prayed. There in the medicine tepee, from under that crude altar, the prayer of the simple man rose to Almighty God. The contents of the medicine man's bundle were placed, again, around the boy—scalp locks, eagle feathers, wing-bone whistles, and human skull. Many Stars and Spirit Wind kept up a low, monotonous chanting; but the doctor wasn't aware of them. He paid no attention to those near him, excepting when he raised his eyes to make some wish known to Bissonette.

White Antelope and her sister, a quiet, intelligent woman, heated stones at the doctor's orders, and chafed Young War Eagle's limbs, as he directed. Once, in the late afternoon, White Antelope's hand touched the boy's head caressingly, brushing back the dark hair. It was a mother-gesture, tender and wistful. Dr. Dean saw then what he had been hoping for. The sick boy's eyelids fluttered. His eyes opened for an instant and closed, wearily. The doctor's heart sang with joy. This was the first evidence of returning consciousness. The death-like sleep that had held Young War Eagle since his fall was loosening its grip.

There was every reason to hope now that the battle would be won. The only wise God had answered the prayers of Dr. Dean.

That night, Dr. Dean stayed with his patient, fearing to trust him even to the care of White Antelope and her sister. He did not trust Many Stars. He thought that he could detect a gleam of jealousy in the old man's ever-watching eyes. Toward morning, the boy opened his eyes again and called his mother by name. White Antelope bent over him, speaking low, what words Dr. Dean did not know. He knew only that they were the right words, for Young War Eagle smiled on hearing them, sighed, and went to sleep. The doctor knew then that the boy would recover. He might leave the medicine tepee and go back to the wagon encampment to rest. White Antelope and her sister, seemingly tireless, would watch. Many Stars, exhausted, slept in a corner of the tepee. He looked more like a brown mummy than a man.

Pale with weariness, Dr. Dean rode back to the encampment, where Bissonette had already given word of the boy's progress. Captain Stephen and Michael came out to meet him, with one question on their lips: "Chief Wolf's Brother ... Myra?" Dr. Dean shook his head.

"I don't know," he answered wearily. "The boy will live, but the chief hasn't said a word to me."

That question remained unanswered for nearly a week.

Captain Stephen had planned to lay over in the shadow of Fort Laramie for only three days—long enough for his people to trade at the fort and rest, before heading out across the desert. The fear of being overtaken by early blizzards in the mountains was what prompted his haste to be on; but the unexpected trouble with which they had met disrupted his good plans. Dr. Dean couldn't leave Young War Eagle until his recovery was well assured. He didn't want to leave until Chief Wolf's Brother had promised that he wouldn't attempt to take Myra. So there was nothing to do but wait.

The captain was worried by the delay. "This is one of the trials of the trail that we didn't count on," he said ruefully to Henri Devine.

"It is," agreed the guide. "And, still, wasn't the boy's accident providential for us? The Dakotas carry out what they have their minds set on ... if they can. Wolf's Brother would have taken Myra Dean even if he had had to massacre the whole outfit to do it."

"And how do we know that he hasn't changed his mind about that?"

Devine was silent. It was true that they had had no pledge of friendship from the chief. The injured boy was making steady improvement. Dr. Dean called to see him every day and waited, hopefully, for a word of

gratitude from Chief Wolf's Brother, a word that did
not come.

⟡ ‡ ⟡

Jerry had spent several hours writing a letter to
Auntie Kay. He had given her the correct information
about Chimney Rock and prairie dogs. Jerry also told
her that they weren't "rockin' mountains" but Rocky
Mountains, and that they never moved and there
was no way of getting round them, for people had to
go over them. His Uncle Jim had taken the letter to
the fort. Some hunter or trapper, going back to the
States, might see that it was delivered to Auntie Kay
in Osage, Missouri.

The little pioneers were enjoying every day of their
stay at Fort Laramie. It was good not to be traveling in the wagon train, and to be able to take deep
breaths without filling the lungs with dust. The air
here was so sweet and clean, and the water was clear
and sparkling—a joy after the muddy, tainted water
of the Platte. On bright days, the snow-mantled tip of
Laramie Peak, one of the highest points in the front
range of the Rockies, dazzled their eyes. All in all, life
around the fort was lively and interesting.

There were campfires in the evenings, too, when
Michael played his flute, and the fiddlers fiddled to
their hearts' content, while the young people danced
and sang. The long-delayed spelling bee was held at
Laramie, and Michael led the hearty cheering when
Laura's little class won over Silas Weeks' older pupils.
Nights of deep, untroubled sleep and days of sheer

pleasure there were for the children, while unknown to them the wagons waited for word from Chief Wolf's Brother.

While they waited, the men and women of the train found much to keep their time occupied. The women washed and patched clothing that was all but worn to shreds, wondering doubtfully whether it would hold out through the mountains. The men repaired wagons, mended torn canvas, replaced iron wagon tires, shoed horses and oxen, molded lead bullets, and cut strips of rawhide and buckskin to make coverings for the oxen's feet. There were sharp rocks ahead, and stone bruises on oxen feet were sometimes little short of tragedies.

The men did brisk trading with the Indians around the fort. They were able to buy some fine buffalo robes, rawhide, and buckskin, in exchange for tobacco and colored beads. Sugar and flour were scarce and almost too expensive to buy, but families did buy some sugar at $1.50 a pint and flour at $40.00 a barrel. Mrs. Stephen drove a good bargain with an Indian woman. She traded two yards of bright calico for a dozen rawhide bags of "wasna," a compound of dried buffalo meat and berries, made as only the Sioux women knew how to make it. This she hid carefully away in the wagon. It would keep for months. Captain Stephen urged the men to lay in a good supply of gunpowder and other ammunition.

"Devine says there will be lots of hunting ahead," the captain said. But he was thinking of Wolf's Brother and his threat.

➤ ✝ ◄

So a week went by, and the Stephen Company could wait no longer. Dr. Dean sought out the chief to take leave of him, taking Bissonette along to interpret for him.

"Young War Eagle will be up and around soon," said Dr. Dean. "My medicine is no longer needed in the camp of Chief Wolf's Brother. I must go with my people, who are anxious to be on the way. They have delayed their journey several days that I might be with the chief's sick son. Tomorrow, at sun-up, we shall take our way on the trail. Good-bye, Chief Wolf's Brother!"

The chief took the doctor's outstretched hand, but he said nothing, and his expression was unreadable. There was a gleam in his eyes, but whether it was friendly or sinister neither Bissonette nor Dr. Dean could tell. White Antelope, though, looked at the doctor as she might have looked at a hero. Indian women were skilled in hiding their emotions, but there was no mistaking the gratitude, the admiration, in the face of Young War Eagle's mother.

"Well, what do you make of that?" exclaimed Dr. Dean, as he and the Frenchman went out of the camp. "What does it mean?"

Bissonette laughed for a moment. "Time will tell!" he said. "It's hard to judge what he has in mind." He was worried.

Dr. Dean felt tired and sick at heart as he rode toward the wagon encampment. Was all his effort in vain? When he slipped wearily from his saddle, Myra left her play and ran to meet him, talking excitedly of the Indian camp that she and Jerry were making from twigs and clay. He laid his hand on her sunny head and spoke cheerily to her; but to himself he groaned, "Myra, child, if we get out of this scrape with our lives—and yours …, I'll see that your hair is dyed as black as midnight!"

❧ ⁜ ☙

That afternoon, Bissonette rode into the wagon camp with a summons from Chief Wolf's Brother. Captain Stephen, Devine, and Dr. Dean went to answer the mysterious order. In reply to the captain's question, Bissonette said that he had no idea what the chief had in mind. He had sent for the men, that was all he could say.

The dark face of Wolf's Brother did not relieve the suspense of the three men when he met them at the entrance to his tepee. The chief was dressed in elegant attire. Captain Stephen was glad that he had taken care to shave and put on a clean shirt. Otherwise, he would have made a sorry figure beside this handsome, carefully-groomed aristocrat of the plains. The three pioneers stood next to the chief's tepee and waited for him to formally welcome them.

Chapter 15

A Chief's Pledge

C hief Wolf's Brother's tepee was the largest and finest in the Dakota camp. Its size told visitors that he was a wealthy man, in the reckoning of his tribesmen, who figured wealth largely in terms of huts and horses. Only an Indian rich in horses could own a large tepee, because a large tepee required many long poles to hold it in place, and many long poles required many strong horses to carry them when camp was being moved. These Plains Indians changed their camp frequently due to the fact that they would often hunt and trap animals to the point where few of them were left to reproduce.

The lodge of the chief, like the lesser lodges, was made of buffalo hide, but his tepee stood out among the others. The hide was cured to a beautiful parchment-like finish and ornamented with brightly-colored figures painted on its mellow surface. The pictures told legends of the chief's family and stories of deeds of the master, himself.

Above the tepee entrance, the chief's medicine bundle was hung—a bag of beaded wolf-skin, wherein were kept articles held in much respect by his family, and thought to bring good fortune to the owners. A lance, thrust into the earth before the tepee, held some of the master's war equipment. It held his shield, artistically made and decorated, his skin quiver of bright-tipped arrows, and his bow all adorned with scalp locks, ermine tails, and war eagle feathers.

A pot that sent up the savory odor of meat and herbs steamed on a bed of coals that burned near the tepee. White Antelope and her sister were busy about the pot. They, like the chief, had dressed, apparently, for an occasion. Their gowns were of soft, white deerskin, trimmed with fringe and colored porcupine quill embroidery. Their moccasins were embroidered likewise, as were the bands that bound their sleek, black heads. No pioneer woman ever took greater pride in her lace and embroidery-making than did these women of the wild plains with their dyed porcupine-quill work. The result of their labor was beautiful.

Standing before his tepee, like a king before his throne, Wolf's Brother greeted his visitors and invited them into his lodging. It was the first time Captain Stephen and Dr. Dean had been in the tepee of a chief, and, anxious though they were, they couldn't resist an interested look around. The place was very clean and orderly. White Antelope was a good housekeeper. The day was warm, so the bottom of the tepee was lifted, allowing the breeze to sweep in. Dr. Dean admired the perfect ventilation of the tepee; the clean, sweet air sweeping in from the bottom, and the heated, impure air escaping through the smoke vent, an opening in the top. The only furnishings were beds made of piles of buffalo robes and back rests of woven willow, covered with robes. Bright bags of deerskin, embellished with tiny shells and the favorite porcupine-quill embroidery, were hung about the tepee. Also, behind the back rest that was clearly that of the chief, so elegantly was it decorated, there was stretched a large piece of tanned hide on which some of the history of his family was painted. Here, too, the coup stick of the chief, decked with elk teeth and ermine tails, was suspended.

The chief seated his guests in a semi-circle about the tepee, indicating where each should sit. Many Stars and Spirit Wind were there, and were seated in

honored places. The faces of the Indians were very solemn. Not a word was spoken. For a moment, after his
guests were placed to his satisfaction, Wolf's Brother
sat motionless, his eyes raised as if in prayer. Then he
gave a signal that must have been for White Antelope
and her sister, for they entered the tepee, carrying a
big pot of steaming meat between them. They placed
it before the chief and laid a pile of bone bowls and a
large bone ladle beside it.

The meat was ladled into the bowls and a bowl
passed to each man. Wolf's Brother, Many Stars, and
Spirit Wind each took a piece of meat from his bowl
and laid it aside—an offering to the spirits. Then the
strange meal was begun, in silence.

"Was this a feast before I meet my end?" Dr. Dean
asked himself the question. He had read once of a
tribe of Indians that feasted its prisoners before put-
ting them to death.

The meat was unlike anything Captain Stephen or
Dr. Dean had ever tasted. It had been cut into small
chunks, and they couldn't tell from its appearance
what it was, but they suspected that they were eating
dog meat. The suspicion didn't add to their already
faint appetites!

Captain Stephen stole a glance at the doctor. He
was eating soberly, as if his life depended upon it, but
his face had a greenish pallor that spoke of nausea. He
looked as if, at any moment, his stomach might throw
out the food that was being forced into it.

The captain braced himself heroically to fight the waves of sickness that swept over him. "It's all a matter of habit!" he told himself, and he recalled that Henri Devine had told him that Indians, eating for the first time what they called "white man's meat"—beef flesh—experienced a similar nausea. When the bowls were empty, the men saw with intense relief that they were not going to be refilled. There was other serious business to be considered.

Chief Wolf's Brother took up his long, finely decorated pipe and filled it carefully with a mixture of tobacco and dried red willow. He placed a tuft of straw on the tobacco and held the pipe out for Many Stars to light. Rising, the chief offered the lighted pipe to the sun, the father of all things, and to the earth, the mother; then he passed it to the guest on his left.

One after the other, each in his turn, the men smoked briefly. They were surprised to see, while the pipe was being passed, that a crowd was gathering outside the tepee. All the men and women of the camp came quietly, their moccasined feet stirring the grass as lightly as wind. They sat on the ground and waited expectantly, those in the foreground peering under the lifted bottom of the tepee.

Captain Stephen and Dr. Dean exchanged nervous glances. Had the Indians gathered to witness their execution? But the voice of the chief commanded their instant attention. Chief Wolf's Brother was speaking in a low, musical voice that was vibrant with emotion. The men were astonished and fascinated by the light that illumined his dark face when he spoke, softening the stern features wonderfully.

Bissonette interpreted the chief's words. "My heart is filled with gratitude to my white brothers who have done for me a service that I can never repay. I and my people will not forget how your great white medicine man came in answer to the prayers of our honored medicine man, Many Stars, and persuaded the Great Spirit to spare the life of my son, Young War Eagle. I will prove to you that a chief does not forget!"

In the silence that followed these words, the chief unwrapped a bundle that Spirit Wind laid before him, and once again the white buffalo robe and the mystic whistle were displayed to the white men. At the same time, a brave approached the tepee leading the beautiful horses that Wolf's Brother had brought to the wagon encampment on that memorable night when he had come to bargain for Myra. The chief resumed his speech. "Accept, White Brothers, these offerings of thanksgiving! They will serve you in your long travel across the desert and through the mountains. The story of your service to Wolf's Brother will run before you like the wind, and these gifts will be a sign to the children of the great Dakota family that you have claim to their friendship."

A low-voiced chorus of approval went up from the listeners outside the tepee.

In the great relief that they felt at the lifting of their long suspense, the visitors had difficulty in replying to Wolf's Brother's courtly speech, but a reply was expected from each of them. So each of them did his best to please. Dr. Dean felt more like giving three cheers than making a formal speech, and Captain Stephen was almost overpowered by the desire to jump on his horse and ride to the wagon encampment with the wonderful news of the chief's gratitude. But the occasion was too solemn for anything but very formal demonstration, and there was much ceremony to be carried out before they could leave the chief's tepee. If Michael had been there, he most certainly would have dumbfounded the Indians by standing on his red head!

After the speeches were made, Captain Stephen presented gifts that he had brought with him— tobacco for the men to mix with their ground red willow, and beads for White Antelope and her sister. Dr. Dean brought the festivity to an end with a prayer and then prepared to leave. Dusk was gathering when the Indians and their new friends parted. After the guests were gone, the voice of Truth Teacher, the old camp crier, echoed through the camp. He walked among the tepees singing a song in praise of the chief's feast.

That night, when the silence of sleep held the Stephen Company, Dr. Dean went to the edge of the camp, where the sentinels kept their solitary watch, and stood for a long time, looking in the direction of Wolf's Brother's circled tepees. There he had fought and won the hardest, strangest battle of his life. He had learned once again to depend on the sovereign grace of God, even in the face of death. Admittedly, he would be leaving the place with many bittersweet memories.

"All's well!" stated the weary guard, as he gave up his post to the midnight relief. This report echoed in the doctor's heart in a mighty big way.

"All's well," thought the doctor. "Thanks be to God, all is well."

Chapter 16

Young Explorers Make a Discovery

Out from Fort Laramie, into the desert, rolled the wagons on a trail that led slowly upward. Day followed day in a procession of travel that became more and more difficult as the desert hemmed the travelers in; a desert of sand and sage, alkali, and rattlesnakes. No Indians molested them, although they heard of clashes between pioneers and Indian raiders. Chief Wolf's Brother was keeping his promise. But there were dangers other than Indians. Barefooted children learned to listen for the peculiar warning of the rattlesnake, made by the rattles on the snake's tail, a sound not unlike that made by rubbing wheat spears together. They learned, too, not to drink from the pools in this region, no matter how thirsty they were, for death lurked in the water. The rotting bodies and wolf-picked skeletons of oxen and horses strewn along

the way were a gruesome warning. Guards were con-
stantly on watch to keep the livestock from the pools,
but in spite of their care some poor, thirst-tormented
animals did make their way to the bad water and drink
their fill. One morning, Michael found three of the
Dean oxen dead. They had been well the evening before.
Others in the company reported animal losses.

Deer Creek, a favorite camping place of the early
trail, was a blessing to the travelers, giving a tempo-
rary relief from thirst. The water in the creek was clear
and pure, and the grass was plentiful on its banks. It
was here, when the wagons made an early afternoon
encampment, that Dan asked permission to give the
boys an exploring trip. He was eager to see for himself
something Henri Devine had told him about. Michael
was busy that afternoon, the youngsters needed a
treat, and the country was safe, so Dan rounded up
Jerry and Jim and four other boys.

"Devine says there used to be a deserted Indian
village around here," he said. "Want to explore it, fellows?"

Dan put his hands over his ears to protect them
from the shout that went up. "Hey! My ears!" he protested. "You boys would wake up the dead!" Then
he laughed, as if a funny thought had struck him.
"Wonder if you could?" he laughed. "Come on!"

He pulled his pistol from the holster at his belt,
examined it, and, satisfied that it was in good con-
dition, slipped the weapon back. He didn't expect to
have to use it, but emigrant boys who were old and

sensible enough to carry firearms usually did carry them. Dan was an expert shot. More than once Jerry and Jim had seen him shoot the head from a coiled rattlesnake. Adventuring with Dan was always fun.

The boys had climbed a rocky, treeless hill and were scanning the country for a trace of the deserted Indian village when they saw, clustered in a sheltered place, a group of tall, skeleton-like structures. From a distance these looked like the pole framework of Indian lodges, but when they had scrambled down the incline and made their way closer, the explorers saw that they were platforms, supported by tall, sturdy poles. There were a dozen platforms, each upheld by four poles, and each bearing a large bundle. The earth beneath the platforms was strewn with glistening bones arranged in designs of circles and stars.

"It looks like Indian work, Dan, but what is it?" asked Jim. "Remember that field all decorated with buffalo bones? Devine said it was an offering to the Great Spirit."

Dan nodded. "And so are these bones an offering to the Great Spirit. I'll tell you fellows what those bundles up there are, if you promise not to get scared. It's pretty spooky!"

"What are they?" chorused the boys.

Dan made his voice hollow and solemn. "Those bundles on the platforms are dead men," he said. "You are standing under the bodies of twelve dead Indians!"

The older boy had to laugh at the expressions on the freckled faces around him.

"Maybe ... maybe we'd better get away from this burial ground," Jerry suggested. "The live Indians might not ... might not like it, if they saw us here."

Dan knew that this was the truth, although he was certain it wasn't exactly why Jerry wanted to be off. Devine had told Dan about this Indian graveyard, and the latter had led the youngsters to it purposely to give them an adventure to thrill them.

The explorers started away, the younger boys tiptoeing, as if they feared to disturb the sleepers on the platforms; but before they had gone far, the air, suddenly grown heavy and oppressive, was torn by a shriek, blood-chilling in its wildness. A human shriek it was, and unmistakably that of an Indian. Then came the throb-throb-throb of a drum, and another yell, and another, each pitched higher than the one it followed. Dan's face paled.

The boys ran ahead, but Dan herded them back.

"Stay here behind this rock!" he commanded. "Don't budge until I tell you to!"

The frightened boys huddled in the shelter of a boulder that shut the open plains from their view, while Dan, his pistol in his hand, crept to the edge of the rock and peered around it. He was amazed by the sight he saw.

Four Indians, dressed only in loin cloths and moccasins, were leaping about on the plains like mad men, beating drums and making furious gestures. Every little while they stopped their wild dancing to shoot an arrow into the air. As he watched in astonishment, Dan could see that there was rhythm and form in their dance.

Puzzled, the boy scanned the sky for sight of a bird at which they might be aiming, but, with the exception of a heavy, black cloud, the sky was empty. There was not a bird in sight.

A rumble of thunder, deep, threatening, sounded, as if some giant beast growled in protest and anger. Then Dan understood. These dancing men were thunder fighters, members of a mystic organization of Plains Indians, thought to have power to ward off thunder and lightning storms. Such storms were greatly dreaded by natives of the open, unsheltered places. A storm was brewing; in fact, it was about to break. The fighters were doing their best to frighten away the great "thunder bird."

Dan would have liked to stay in this secluded spot and watch the contest between the Indians and the thunder gods, but he dared not expose the boys to the fury of an electric storm in the open. He turned back to the explorers, who were watching him with owl-like eyes. Then a mischievous thought popped into Dan's head. The boys had come out for a thrill. He would give them one that they wouldn't forget soon.

He whispered hoarsely, "Come on, fellows! We've got to run!" He made for the wagon encampment, the boys tearing along at his heels, thinking that they were running from a pack of warpath Indians.

Their exploring trip was an adventure that they didn't forget soon, and one that they agreed, afterward, they wouldn't have missed. It was part of the toughening process that made small emigrant boys like Jerry able to meet danger and trial with almost grown-up endurance.

❦ ‡ ❦

Good-bye, now, to the North Platte, followed so long! As they wheeled on into the desert country, the wagons passed dry beds of alkali lakes, where the ground was white with glistening powder. To the children, the silvery covering, spreading far and wide, looked like a fresh fall of snow, soft and cool; but it was pleasing in looks only. The powder ate into the skin, and bathing only added to the torment, for water and alkali dust mixed made a lye solution. When Jerry struggled to keep from crying over his burned feet at night, his aunt struggled to keep from crying, too. She treated the sore skin with melted buffalo tallow, and, when he had fallen to sleep, Beth Stephen's tears did fall as she looked at the small, swollen feet that had still so far to go.

Warnings left by thoughtful travelers were posted by many pools. Some of the warnings were printed on pieces of cloth and tied to bushes or stakes driven into the ground. Others were penciled on bleached buffalo and oxen skulls. The words were few:

BEWARE! POISON WATER!

In spite of the warning, some of the Stephen people tried to satisfy their thirst in the pools, and there was much sickness as a result. Stomach aches and sore mouths made many miserable, and it was not long before Dr. Dean used up his supply of stomach remedies.

Myra cried for water, and Jerry looked longingly at every pool they passed.

"We'll be reaching the Sweetwater soon," said Captain Stephen. "Then you may drink the river dry."

The Sweetwater would soon be in sight! The promising name of the desert river rang like a song in the minds of the weary, thirsty children. Jerry wondered if the water would be sweet, like sugar, and he hoped that it wouldn't. Just plain water would be better, he thought ... just plain cold water. When they reached, at last, the longed-for river, a shallow stream that ran gently over the sands, they threw themselves down on their stomachs, put their mouths in the water, and drank with long, hungry sucks, as animals do. They had known long before they reached the river that they were near one. The mules, scenting water, had set up a braying that nearly deafened everyone.

Not many miles from where they hit the Sweetwater was Independence Rock, a famous trail landmark. It stood, as it stands today—a great, solid piece of granite, shaped, one trail historian has said, "like a giant tortoise, forever fixed on the floor of the plains." The names of thousands of overland travelers were cut or painted on its broad surface—those of famous explorers, along with those of no less heroic, though unknown, pioneers. Michael was kept busy helping the children to imprint their names on this "great register of the desert," as it was called by those who had gone before. Deeply into the granite they cut them and filled the letters with tar. Myra wanted Annabelle's name beneath hers, but Annabelle was such a long name! Michael suggested that they abbreviate it to Anna, and Myra was satisfied with that option.

Emigrants who reached Independence Rock around the Fourth of July stayed encamped there to celebrate their country's birthday. Captain Stephen threw the children into raptures by promising them a celebration on the morrow. The men and women stayed up late that night planning the celebration. The children, they said, had earned a day of fun. The truth be told, they all had earned a day of relaxation. The decision to stop for a day was never easy, however, for all the adults knew that they had to make it through the mountains before the heavy snows or perish!

Chapter 17

Fourth of July in the Desert

Crack! Crack! Crack! The smart report from the sentinels' rifles firing a military salute awakened the sleepers to the glad realization this was the Fourth of July, their day of celebration. The children sprang up and pulled on their clothes. They couldn't miss a minute of this joyous holiday in the desert. Sounding closely after the military salute came a bugle call and roll of drums.

"Hey, Jerry! Listen to that!" Jim's eyes were shining. He was so excited that he put his shirt on inside out!

Proudly through the clear desert air Michael's flute began to sing. It was like a human voice calling to them, stirring their blood, quickening their hearts. The boys scrambled from under the wagon where they had slept and stood at attention, listening:

"Oh, say, can you see,
By the dawn's early light,
What so proudly we hailed
At the twilight's last gleaming?"

Michael's flute was singing their country's grand song. Heard here in the wilderness, in the shadow of the mighty mountains, so far, so very far from any place that they could call home, there was something tremendous about it—something that roused the heart with patriotic pride.

Jim felt the smart of tears in his eyes and an ache in his throat. He wasn't the only one so affected. His father stood, unashamed, with tears on his cheeks, and other men wiped their faces with the backs of work-toughened hands.

Fiddles and harmonicas joined with the flute. The voices of the emigrants took up the song, and the air rang with the triumphant words:

"'Tis the star-spangled banner—
Oh, long may it wave
O'er the land of the free
And the home of the brave!"

So the glad day was begun. There was speechmaking at noon and a banquet of dried buffalo meat boiled with rice as the main dish, with cold sliced cornmeal mush and molasses for dessert. Never was any banquet more enjoyed.

"Will you wait until dark for the fireworks?" asked Captain Stephen, with a twinkle in his eyes.

"Fireworks! Fireworks!" the children shouted. They could scarcely believe their ears. And then, "No! We want them now! Now!" they cried.

It was a fortunate decision for the Stephen Company.

Michael and Dan rolled out a small keg of powder and set it up at a safe distance from the crowd of interested watchers. An excited buzz went up: "A keg of powder!"

Michael had fastened a piece of tarred rope in the bunghole of the barrel. He set fire to the free end and ran away. The rope sputtered and burned toward the keg.

"Do you think there's really powder in it?" Jerry wondered.

"Of course, there is! What'd be the sense of firing an empty keg? Father said we'd have fireworks. You just wait and see!"

"Wow! It'll rock the big rock when it goes off. Look—"

Myra held Annabelle protectingly close. She covered the doll's head carefully with her little shawl. Slowly, slowly the sputtering fire crept toward the keg. The children held their breath. Would the fire go out before it reached the keg?

No—it had reached it now … sputter, sputter … Bang!

The explosion didn't rock Independence Rock, but it was loud enough to satisfy the hearts of the children. They were running to investigate the spot where the keg had been when a warning shout stopped them. Everyone stopped, laughter ceased, and all became tensely alert. The guards were shooting at something. Swift, dark figures were darting away into the distance.

"What are they? Animals?"

"No! They're humans … Indians, they must be!"

The camp was in an uproar of excitement. Where had the prowlers come from? Had they risen from the earth? The country was level for a good distance around, and there was little growth on it, only scattered clumps of greasewood sage and cactus. How had anyone come so close without being seen? It was a mystery that there was no time for the guards to solve then, for another startling thing claimed attention. From the outskirts of the corral, where they had been picketed, a dozen horses started for liberty, their ropes dangling. They had been cut loose.

"After them! Head them off and get them back!"

Then it was that the gift horses of Chief Wolf's Brother proved their worth. Fleet, obedient to every command of their riders, trained by master horsemen, they made after the frightened animals, caught up with them, hemmed them in, and turned them back to the corral. Wolf's Brother had spoken truly of these horses: "They will serve you in your long travel across the desert."

Unerringly, the thieves had picked the best animals. They had planned to mount them and make a dashing getaway, a daring scheme that might have worked if the exploding powder keg had not thrown them into a panic. It was clear that they had been watching the wagon train for some time. Perhaps they had lain in wait all night, watching for an opportunity to get at the horses. The guard had been relaxed for the celebration, the opportunity the Indians had awaited. Imperceptibly, they must have moved their thin bodies along the brown earth, knives ready to cut the horses' ropes and to pierce the hearts of the guards, if the need arose. Now it was clear. They had new enemies to face.

"They must be Arapahoes, or maybe they are Comanches," said Henri Devine. "Sly as foxes when it comes to stealing horses, and as mean as they can be."

"From now on, we will travel under double guard," declared Captain Stephen.

The wagons traveled as quietly as possible all the way up the Sweetwater Valley, and though they met no more threatening Indians, they didn't relax their guard. They knew that there was danger in this region of coming into contact with groups of warriors making their way down from the hills, or up from the plains, to carry on their customary warfare over the buffalo, one tribe against another. When the heat and drought of summer sent the giant plains animals to the uplands to find fresh grass and untainted water, the Native American hunters followed them, and bloody battles were fought   between rival

tribes. Horses were needed for these battles, and the horses of wagon caravans were a constant source of temptation. The Stephen Company had been warned at Independence Rock.

Across the Sweetwater splashed the wagons and the long lines of livestock, and out to a narrow canyon, called "Devil's Gate," they made their way, where God had cut a chasm four hundred feet deep through a mountain of solid granite. Through this great gap the country that lay beyond could be seen for a distance of ten miles. A marvelous sight it was, a glimpse to the travelers of the rocky wilderness that lay before them.

Jim wondered why the place had been called "Devil's Gate," since the Sweetwater flowed through it so quietly and calmly.

Jim's father said, "According to Shoshone legend, a powerful evil spirit in the form of a great beast cut through that mountain of rock to escape the attack of brave Indian warriors. But in truth, Son, God formed that narrow passage."

Jerry was glad, too, to find out that Devil's Gate wasn't what he had expected to find. The dreadful name had called up memories of Auntie Kay's stories of the place of punishment where, she had declared, boys who ran away from home, told lies, stole, or swore would certainly wind up. He hadn't confessed it to anyone, but he had been dreading this "Devil's Gate." He had been fearing to come to massive iron doors, with smoke and flames rising from behind them, and the brimstone of Auntie Kay's stories filling the air with biting fumes. He sniffed testingly. No smoke or brimstone was in sight! This air was clean and sweet and bracing. It made a boy want to throw back his shoulders and fill his lungs to bursting.

The wagons rounded Devil's Gate and made their way to the bank of the river, where camp was made for the night. In the morning, they would take up the climb that would lead them through the South Pass to the summit of the Continental Divide. Not many more days of travel and the desert with its cactus thorns, burning alkali dust, and poisoned water would be a memory, as the plains and prairies had already become. The giant arms of the Rockies were opening to gather in their company. As always, it was forward march, one day at a time.

Chapter 18

Cavaliers of the Rockies

"Indians coming this way!" The warning of the guards rang along the line of wagons.

Captain Stephen and Henri Devine went to join the guards outside the wagon barricade. Every man reached for his rifle. The mothers herded the children into the wagons. The waiting hush with which the emigrants prepared for the striking of an enemy fell upon the encampment now. But, at their place before the barricade, the captain and the guide were having an argument.

"They aren't Indians," Devine was insisting. "There are only seven of them. Seven Indians wouldn't dare attack a wagon train."

"But surely they are!" Captain Stephen protested. "Did you ever see anyone but an Indian ride like that? Look, man! They're turning back! No—they're coming on again, right at us! What sort of tactics are those, anyway?"

Devine laughed. "Crazy men!" he muttered. "You wait, Captain! You watch this!"

Before the captain knew what he was about to do, Devine leaped on a horse and rode out toward the strangers, yelling savagely. He took his kerchief from about his neck and waved it above his head as he rode.

The oncoming horsemen reined their horses to a standstill and waited. Then Devine seemed to go crazy. He whooped in a perfect imitation of an Indian war whoop, fired his pistol into the air, and made his horse rear and balk, run in circles, prance forward, backward, sideways—do everything but stand on its head. Watching him in blank amazement, his companions thought the guide had taken leave of his senses.

"Hurry, we'll have to rope him and pull him in, poor creature!" shouted Michael. "He's out of his head, entirely. 'Tis the heat has done it!"

But Devine's antics had a curious effect on the strangers. They watched him in silence for a while, and then, with roars of laughter, they rode to him and formed a circle about him. Captain Stephen knew then that they were not Indians. Indians didn't laugh like that. They were white men, as Devine had insisted, and, after greeting them heartily, the guide led them to the captain.

"Tell the men to put down their rifles," he called out, "and let the women and children come out and finish their suppers. These men are friends, free trappers ... and they wouldn't hurt a fly!"

The women came out, indignant, but greatly relieved.

"It's a mercy they weren't shot, acting like that!" they whispered to one another, but they soon forgot their resentment in the interest of watching these strange men who looked so much like Indians.

The trappers wore their hair long, braided tightly with colored ribbons. Their skin was weathered to a copper color. Their shirts of embroidered buckskin, their hair-leggins, their beaded moccasins, their bright sashes in which were fastened pistols, knives, and Indian pipes all fascinated the youngsters. These were like story-book men—cavaliers of the mountains.

The trappers were timid, at first, in the presence of the emigrants, and tongue-tied as bashful children. After they had eaten the food the women put before them and smoked a pipe with the men, they forgot their uneasiness and talked freely. They were hungry for the sight of city folk, although by choice they had left civilization for life in the wilds, married Indian women, and given themselves over to Indian habits and customs. For the most part, they were American men, although a couple were French-Canadians. They were eager, therefore, to spend a few hours with American families, speaking the English language and hearing it spoken.

These Rocky Mountain trappers were adventurers, who had lived fifteen years or more in the mountain wilds. These men knew that region of deep canyons, blind valleys, narrow trails that zigzagged up and down sheer precipices, raging summer torrents, and snowbound winter passes, as other men knew favorite books. Their senses were trained to a sharpness keener than the senses of the animals they trailed and trapped. Their lives depended on those senses.

One of the men, named Jules, had somber, brooding eyes and a face so horribly scarred that it frightened the children. Louis was the spokesman of the group; Henry walked with a limp, the souvenir of a fight with a pack of wolves; Edward and Francis were twin brothers; Jean was a small, thin fellow, with a face as sharp as a fox's face; and Connel was soft-spoken and gentle in manner.

They were free trappers; that is, men who worked at trapping for themselves, unattached to any of the fur-trading companies that had been doing a thriving business in the country for years. They lived lives of solitude, trapping and hunting through the snowbound winter months, when the fur of animals was at its best, and coming out of their seclusion rarely. Until recently, they had come together annually at a summer rendezvous: trappers and hunters, Indian and white, and rival traders. At this famous summer gathering, the pelts that the trappers had risked their lives to gather were exchanged for supplies, and a month of bargaining and celebration held sway. The daring day of the trapper was fast becoming a thing of the past as the covered wagons, like those of the Stephen train, rolled into the West and brought an end to the solitude. The secret, cunning trails of the wilderness men—which, with wild animal and Indian trails, were the first in the West—were being wiped out; silk hats were taking the place of felt hats made from beaver fur, and trapping was no longer the profitable business it had been.

The boys of the Stephen Company sat with the men that night, listening to the trappers' stories of their adventures trailing fur-bearing animals and game in the mountains, and learning about the country into which they were going. They gathered around a big bed of coals that was not allowed to flame high for fear of attracting enemies. It was at this gathering that Jerry and Jim, with the other boys and men, heard such tales as they had never heard before.

Poor Jules bore proof of his closest escape from death in his terribly scarred face.

"Jules, here, he come face to face weeth a bear," said Louis, jerking the long stem of his Indian pipe toward his unfortunate companion. "De bear, did not like hees face, so she make it over! Quick as you please, she slap heem in de face, and, presto! Jules' own mother she would not know heem!"

Louis laughed as if he had told a good joke, but the listeners were shocked. Pity for the mutilated man, who they felt must be suffering from this brutally frank discussion of his disfigurement, held them silent. But they were mistaken. Jules didn't mind. His brooding eyes flamed with a curious light. He took his pipe from his lipless mouth and smiled gamely. "But, yes, yes! Go on, Louis! What Jules do to dat bear? You tell dat, too, mebbee? Eh?"

"Tell it yourself, Jules! You tell it!" The demand went up from everyone, and Jerry and Jim edged closer. Then Jules told his story and carried the eager campfire group with him as he spoke.

Jules explained that the winter trapping was over, and the warmth of summer was waking the mountains from sleep. Streams that had been held in frozen dumbness through long months leaped now in roaring torrents down the crags. The trappers gathered together the pelts that they had cached during the season. They were on their way to the yearly rendezvous in Pierre's Hole, a favored meeting place that lay in a valley shadowed by three towering peaks—the Three Tetons. Payment and a long-awaited holiday were at hand.

Over the long, steep slopes of the mountains rode the trappers, their trained mounts picking a precarious footing along the narrow paths. This caravan had long strings of packhorses, laden with pelts and supplies, following. Hard travel, it was. Now they must fight their way through a torrent; now they must chop a passage through a barricade of windfalls; now they must build a road for the horses' feet. From all sides trappers were coming to the yearly rendezvous.

Jules was famed, even among mountain men, as a path-breaker. This day he, being the leader of his group, rode well ahead of the line, along the edge of a precipice. It was nearing the day's close, and mountain men didn't like ledges after daylight. Yet Jules told himself that a camping place must be near. Ah, yes, he remembered well, there was one just around the boulder ahead. But he recalled that the path was dangerously narrow there. Best to dismount and go on foot, he thought. So he got off his horse and started around the boulder.

The horse drew back with a sharp snort of fear. Jules's hand flew to the pistol at his belt. A grizzly bear thrust its muzzle almost into his face. Like a flash, its paw shot out and swiped the pistol from Jules's hand, even as he fired. The weapon fell into the canyon. The terrified horse lost its footing and crashed to its death. The man and an enraged mother bear were face to face on a narrow ledge with a bottomless ravine below.

The bear struck out again. Jules tried to dodge the blow, but its sharp claws caught his face, tearing the flesh from forehead to chin. He threw up his hand and dashed the blood from his eyes. Then, keener than the pain that seared him, was the joy he knew—he was not blinded. His eyes remained.

Those eyes flashed now, as the Frenchman relived the terrible moments. He leaped to his feet, snatched the long knife from his belt, and crouched low in the

firelight. His mutilated face, convulsed with rage, was hardly human—it seemed a dreadful mask. His voice rose to a shriek. "Then Jules get mad! He say, I show you, Mrs. Bear! Jules show you!"

He made a powerful upward thrust, the blade of his knife flashing; then another and another. "Ah-h-h!" His low snarl was like that of a beast, and Jerry took tight hold of Jim's arm. Jules might have been actually fighting again that battle on the mountain ledge, so vividly did he enact the scene. Slowly he drew the knife down, as if he were again pulling it from the heart of his wild attacker. He wiped the blade on his hair-fringed leggins and thrust the weapon back into his belt.

"So!" he concluded. "Madame Bear, she tumble down ... down—"

He put his hands to his forehead and drew them down over his face where his nose and lips should have been. He laughed a hard laugh and shrugged. "Yes, sir!" he admitted. "Dat bear, she do tings to Jules's face—but what happened to de bear?"

Jerry shivered and glanced over his shoulder. It was dark back there ... and they were not far from those same mountains!

Then it was Henry's turn, he with the lame leg, to tell how he had faced a pack of ravenous wolves after a long, losing run through deeply-drifted snow; how, at bay, brought to a standstill when one of his snow shoes broke, he had battled with them, beating them off with his rifle butt when he could fire no more; how his brother trappers, waiting for his return, and hearing his screams and the howls of the wolves, had come in time to save his life, but not before the tendons of one leg had been snapped by one of the heinous creatures that had made its way up behind him while he fought with the pack in front.

Not all trappers and mountain men were so fortunate as Jules and Henry. There were blood-chilling accounts of cruel deaths in the bitter wilderness, stories that haunted the boys' dreams for nights. And there were inspiring tales of remarkable men of that remarkable period, whom the trappers knew personally. The little pioneers thrilled to accounts of the adventures of Jim Bridger, foremost of mountain men, whom they hoped to see soon, when their wagons reached his fort and trading post. They heard of Kit Carson, daring and cool-headed scout and guide, even then acting as guide to an expedition of the explorer, John Charles Fremont; of Thomas Fitzpatrick, gallant young Irishman, feared and respected by the Indians, who called him "Bad-Hand" because of his crippled hand and sometimes "White Hair" because of his hair that had turned prematurely gray after a gruesome experience with the Blackfeet. They marveled over Jedediah Smith, brave explorer and trapper, whose short, splendid life was like a drama, and who had been killed by Comanche Indians in the Cimarron Desert when he had stooped to drink from a pool he had scooped in the sand. But it was the story of John Colter and his race for life that sank deepest into Jim's mind. He was never to forget it.

Louis told the story in his rapid, broken English, resorting to a phrase in French, now and then, or a word of Indian jargon, where his English failed him; but his listeners, alert with interest, were able to follow him. His brother trappers, too, listened as closely as if they were hearing of the dauntless Colter for the first time, although they knew the story all by heart. It was old, old to them—a trapper tradition to be handed down the years. Dark eyes gleaming, white teeth flashing, quick hands gesturing, they listened, interrupting Louis at times with excited comments or additions to his tale. It wasn't often they found an audience like this one!

Colter, an American, Louis explained, was a true man of the mountains, fearless and strong, quick as the lightning in wit. He had served for three years with the famous exploring expedition of Lewis and Clark early in the nineteenth century—no unbroken trail was too wild for John Colter—and when he had asked for his release from the explorers to go into trapping, they had let him leave with regret. He had served them well. True, people laughed at him when he told of certain wonderlands he had found in his lonely exploring trips. "Colter's Hell" they named one region that he described. They scoffed at what later they found to be true, as they had laughed when Colter declared that the Rockies could be crossed with wagons. But, such ridicule did not matter! The explorer slipped away into the great silence to trap for himself. Then came the Spaniard, Manuel Lisa, head of a fur-trading group, asking Colter's help.

Manuel was having trouble of his own with the Crow Indians. He wanted their friendship, which he couldn't gain. Would Colter go among these Indians, win their confidence, and make them know that their trade was wanted by the white traders? No one else in all the country could do it. Into the dangerous Crow territory Colter went, alone, and the suspicious Indians gave their hearts to him.

But there was trouble in store for the fearless one. Before he could get back home, warfare broke out between the Blackfeet and the Flatheads. The Crows came to the help of the gallantly fighting Flatheads, who were greatly outnumbered by the ferocious Blackfeet. Blackfeet braves fell thick and fast under the clever Crow fire; but the Blackfeet did not lay their defeat to the Crows. No. It was the white man,

Colter, that they blamed. He had led their enemies. They vowed to make him pay for the Blackfeet loss. It was after the mountain man had gone back to his free trapping that they found their chance. The Indian memory is long!

Colter, with a companion, John Potts, who had also served with Lewis and Clark, was trapping on a narrow side stream of the Jefferson River one day when the Blackfeet made good their threat. He knew that he was a hunted man, so he worked with great caution. Always, in this region, he set his traps and gathered them at night. The Blackfeet were not abroad near the Jefferson at night. The river was haunted after sundown, the wise ones said, and the Indians, who had no fear of human enemies, were mortally afraid of the supernatural. Silently, the trappers' canoe glided through the dark water. The trapping was good here. They must place all their traps. In their deep interest, they overstayed their time. Daybreak found them still on the river, and so did the Blackfeet!

The moccasined feet, creeping stealthily through the shadows, gave no warning, until, suddenly—what was that rushing, muffled sound? Not thunder, not buffalo—Colter's instinct warned him. He was not surprised to see the shore on either side of the stream come to life, aswarm with Blackfeet, his enemies who hated him.

The trappers' eyes swept the army of Blackfeet warriors. There were at least five hundred of them, standing there in the gray dawn-light, armed with spears, tomahawks, clubs, and bows and arrows. There was no escape. Swiftly as the lightning runs, so ran Colter's thought. There might be a chance. Indians admired courage. It would be best to face them fearlessly. He brought the canoe to shore, stepped out, and urged his companion to come with him. But Potts would not. He knew the danger, he said. Better instant death than capture and torture. He thrust his paddle against the shore and pushed out into midstream. An arrow followed and struck him. Colter called for his friend to come back. Instead, Potts lifted his rifle and fired. An Indian fell dead. Instantly, the trapper was pierced by dozens of arrows. His day was over.

Now they would deal with Colter, friend of their enemies. The trapper faced them patiently and quietly. An Indian wrenched his rifle from his hands. Others stripped every bit of clothing from him. They meant to torture him then. Colter drew his fine body up straight and folded his arms across his chest. He listened while they talked of how they should kill him. Should they set him up as a target and see how many arrows and spears he could hold? That would be good practice for the young warriors. They talked of other methods of vengeance. Ah, but the Blackfeet could be cruel!

The young men were eager for their sport with the captive. But wait, said the older, wiser ones; this was a man of bravery. They would test his spirit. They would let him race with death, and they would give him a few yards' lead. That tribute the Blackfeet would pay to courage.

Colter's heart leaped when he heard this, for he was a swift runner. If the Blackfeet let him go without maiming him, he might win the race with death. The fleetest young runners of the band were singled out. They set their captive in the lead, and then, with deafening yells, they made after him. The race was on.

Six miles of open plains lay between Colter and the river where he might find safety. Six miles' worth of danger! Could he make it? Ah, what a test that was!

Never had Colter run as he ran then. Thorns and rocks cut his bare feet to the bone. Blood gushed from his nose and mouth and streamed down his body. Pain tore his lungs. The yells behind him were getting dimmer, it seemed. Was he outdistancing his enemies or was the dimming of their voices due to his failing senses? He dared a glance over his shoulder, and saw that he had left all but one Indian far behind. That one was on his heels, not fifty feet away—gaining—Colter's sharp wit flashed. There was an ancient Indian ruse—his last hope. He would make use of it. With a cry, he wheeled, arms thrown high above his head, and faced the man at his heels. Startled, the Blackfoot stopped short, stumbled, and fell. The spear bounded from his hand. Colter snatched it and thrust it through the fallen warrior's heart. After taking the Indian's blanket, he was off and away!

The river, the river—through a veil of darkness that threatened to blind him, he could see it, a gleam of promise, beckoning him on. He drove his quivering limbs and bursting lungs to one last mighty effort. As soon as he reached the spot, he fell down the bank and into the water. The cold shock revived him. He swam to one of the many piles of driftwood and brush that lined the river shore and came up under its shelter for rest and breath.

All that day the Blackfeet swarmed around looking for the man who had dropped so mysteriously out of sight—but they didn't find him. After nightfall, when they had left the river, Colter swam down the Jefferson and made his way to shore. He struggled across land and water for seven nights, hiding away like an animal in the daytime, nearly naked and unarmed, with no food but leaves and roots, until he came to the fort of his friend, Manuel Lisa, on the Bighorn. They didn't know him, his friends at the fort, so worn and wild he appeared. They didn't believe his story, at first. They thought it the raving of a sick man. But they found that it was true, every word of it.

Louis, his story at an end, drew a long puff on his pipe and looked around the campfire group. Silence held the men and boys.

"Was he not a man of courage, this Colter? No?" the trapper asked.

"He was a man of courage," Captain Stephen answered. The captain spoke softly, his eyes on Jim's face. The boy was looking out toward the mountains, and his face held the rapt expression of one who sees a vision.

"I'll bet he never went back to that place on Jefferson Fork where the Blackfeet caught him!" said Dan.

A chorus of laughter went up from the trappers.

"But you are wrong!" cried Louis. "What you tink a good trapper like this Colter let his best traps go like dat? No, no! He go back after his traps; but—" Louis shook his head mournfully— "his very fine traps, dey were gone."

Jim lay awake a long time that night thinking of John Colter. Louis had told them that Colter was no longer living. It was too bad a man like that had to die, the boy thought. He was to learn that such a man does not ever really die. His courage inspires other men, and, in them, his spirit lives on. Jim was to have good reason to recall Colter and his clever ruse before many days had passed.

Chapter 19

Shadows Gather

"We are climbing through the South Pass, a long, natural path through the Rocky Mountains. The climb is very gradual. We hardly know that we are climbing … but the oxen know it! Their loads must be lightened."

So Captain Stephen wrote in his journal, a daily record of the trail.

The oxen did know that they were climbing. Worn and thin from the long travel, the toiling beasts plainly showed the strain of the ascent. To relieve the strain, wagon contents were sorted over once more, and some of the big prairie schooners were lightened by cutting out a section of the wagon box. Spinning wheels fell beside cradles in the South Pass; pots and pans and iron ovens joined the debris of the trail. Not infrequently, a broken wagon lying forlornly by the rocky way, the tattered remnants of its canvas cover marked with the brave inscription, "TO OREGON," flapping dismally in the wind, told of someone's loss.

An old German blacksmith, Hans Sommer, wept because he had to throw away a steel anvil and a grindstone in the pass. Jerry thought it very sad to see the old man wringing his hands and crying over the tools.

"Ach! Verloren! Verloren!" the blacksmith kept saying over and over. "Lost! Lost!"

Jerry stared at the anvil and grindstone. They didn't seem worth all those tears.

"Why does he feel so bad, Jim?" he whispered. "Can't he get others in Oregon?"

"Well," Jim answered shortly. "Anvils and grindstones don't grow on bushes."

Other tools from other wagons went out to keep the German's lost ones dreary company. Here and there, a plow was unlashed from the tailboard of a battered wagon. Dr. Dean put out a box of medical books. He threw away his precious books, but he closed his eyes to the little mahogany cradle. It would not have to go—yet.

Some of the men were binding their oxen's hoofs with buckskin and rawhide. "Oxen moccasins," Myra called them, and she declared that they should be beaded.

"Oh, no!" laughed Michael. "Beaded, is it? The creatures would be puttin' on such airs there'd be no gettin' them to move, at all! Well, we might have to go 'round scratchin' their noses the way we have to scratch Beauty's ... the spoiled scalawag!"

Myra was delighted with this quaint and funny idea of Michael's. Laughing, she ran to tell her mother about it. Looking after her, Michael's face lost its smile. Poor wee colleen, he thought. This trail was too long and hard for children.

❖ ‡ ❖

Finally, one evening, Captain Stephen wrote happy lines in his journal. The lines were almost like a song of triumph:

"This day we reached the summit of South Pass. We are, at last, on top of the Continental Divide, on the ridge that separates the waters flowing into the Atlantic Ocean from those flowing into the Pacific— the Indians' Everywhere-Salt-Water. We will go on down the pass now, on the western side of the Rockies. Although we are but half way to our destination, Oregon lies before us. The country from here to the Pacific is Oregon country."

From the top of South Pass the emigrants had nothing to tell them that they were on the top of the Rockies. They saw only a broad, plain-like horizon;

but later they had a view that took their breath away. Snow peaks pierced the skies with eternally icy tips; valleys played hide and seek with one another among the towering crags of ranges. Powerful rivers, which looked like silver ribbons from that height, rushed to the Pacific Ocean. Green River Valley, famous rendezvous place of mountain men, stretched out before their marveling eyes. Now, for the first time, a true sense of the vastness, the wildness of the West into which they were going, gripped the children. They felt very small.

One night they camped on Pacific Spring, which poured its crystal waters into the Green River, the upper portion of the Colorado, called Seedskedee by the Indians. Wild sage grew everywhere. It filled the clear mountain air with its spicy fragrance. Campfires had to be watched carefully here, for the pitchy, dry sage burned wildly. In the evenings, ravens croaked about the camp, and the children saw slinking shapes in the shadows, the shapes of wolves, waiting a chance to prowl. When the wagons pulled away, they would swarm over the abandoned camp in search of scraps and refuse. The guards watched closely to keep the gray hordes from raiding the livestock corral. Wolves had a trick of sneaking down among the horses, gnawing the ropes that tied them, and driving the frightened animals away to a place where the wolves could safely kill and devour them.

There were, in truth, bears in the rocky caverns now. No need to make believe. Dan shot one, and the camp had a supper of bear meat. Bighorn sheep, swift and sure of foot, were seen every day, making their nimble way to the tops of peaks. The hunters fired at them, but their shots were wasted. These bighorns seemed to have charmed lives.

As the trail had been a climb for many days, it now became a gradual decline, with the wagons rolling down the western slopes of the mountains. Out through the Green River Desert they went, splashing their way through the two Sandys, branches of the Green River, and fording that swiftly-rushing, icy water in safety.

"Heaven's star is shining on us!" declared Captain Stephen after they had crossed the Green. "I heard from some traders that seven men were drowned at this crossing last week."

The captain had heard something more from the traders, something that put the men of the company on guard. A party of Blackfeet had made a raid on a wagon train in the neighborhood of Black's Fork, a branch of the Green River, not far away. The Indians were out for horses, and scalps, too, if they could get them.

"Yore horses'll look mighty good to them Blackfeet," the traders had predicted. "Got some goodlookin' animals in that outfit."

❖ ‡ ❖

It was in the neighborhood of the raid that an unfortunate accident happened. One of the Stephen Company men, chasing an antelope, fired into a thicket where he had seen his quarry take refuge. He was horrified to hear a human yell of anguish. He ran to the thicket and found there an Indian, writhing in a death struggle. The shot had struck his temple. He died while the hunter was lifting him from the ground.

"He shouldn't have been in the thicket," one of the men protested. "Look, he had his bow and arrows handy! What was he doing, spying on us?"

Devine shook his head. "Maybe he was spying," he said, "but it is far more likely that he was only hunting. Why didn't you clearly mark and identify your target before you fired? It was an accident, of course, but can we make his people believe that?"

They couldn't. There was an uproar when the slain Indian's companions learned of his death. It was plain to see that they were more enraged than grieved; and it was evident to the men, who were guilty of being careless, that the Indians would have taken swift vengeance if they had not been so outnumbered.

Devine did his best to convince them that the unfortunate happening was an accident, but they met his explanation with a stony silence. To show his company's regret, Captain Stephen chose a good young horse and offered it to the dead man's brother. The scowling Indian examined the horse swiftly. He accepted it with sullen mutterings, and he was still muttering when he rode away carrying the body of his brother. The pioneers watched the Indians go, in silence.

"Unfortunate!" said Henri Devine, finally.

A raven flew overhead. Its hoarse cry seemed to prophesy evil. Captain Stephen shivered and wondered why. It was as if a chilling shadow had fallen between him and the sun.

Chapter 20

Blackfoot Reprisal

B ridger's trading post stood in the valley of Black's Fork, a beautiful spot, green and inviting. Jim Bridger had built the post in 1843, when, to his way of thinking, the old West was a thing of the past. Her free spirit, he declared, was broken. Civilization had taken the reins in her hands, and the beautiful wild country was fast becoming as tame as a kitten. The day of the trapper was over, and Bridger, who had made the secret trails of the wilderness his footpaths, was trying vainly to resign himself to trading with emigrants in a log house by the side of the wagon road. Very often, chafing under the restraint, he was off and away, and his post was closed, much to the disgust of covered wagon travelers who stopped there, hoping to buy supplies.

The post, or fort, which was soon to become famous, was nothing much to look at. Several rudely-built log cabins, plastered from ground to roof with adobe mud that the sun baked to rocky hardness, made up the station "shacks." Regardless of how humble these dwellings were, the shacks of Bridger's post were a welcome sight to the wilderness-wearied travelers. They offered the first real resting place west of the Rockies.

Usually when they reached this spot the emigrants' clothing was in tatters and their cupboards were quite bare. If Jim Bridger or his partner, Louis Vasquez, were

at home, the travelers could stock up on foodstuffs
and clothing, and have their animals shod and their
wagons overhauled. Letters could be left here, too,
with a reasonable hope that eastward-bound traders
or hunters would carry them back to the old home.
Jerry sent a note to Auntie Kay, in one of his uncle's
letters. It read:

> Dear Auntie Kay: I am a real big boy now, and
> my Sunday pants are all wore out, but its all right
> because my old pants don't fit so well anyway. I saw
> the devils gate and there was not any fire or brim-
> stone. Not even a devil around. But I still say my
> prayers anyway. Us fellows are not afraid of bears
> or injuns or anything else I guess. I am not much
> afraid of devils anymore. Hoping you are the same,
> I am, yours truly, Jerry. I still love you.

X.

Jerry was, indeed, a big boy now, scornful of rocking chairs and lullabies. His letter told the truth when
it described his pants as all worn out. Aunt Beth
declared that she would buy buckskin trousers for
Jerry and Jim at Fort Bridger, if they were for sale.
The boys hoped that there wouldn't be any for sale.
Buckskin trousers were mighty uncomfortable things
to wear when it rained. They held water as a sponge
does, and dried as stiff as a board. If a fellow happened to be sitting when his buckskin trousers dried,
he could hardly bend his knees when he stood. The
trousers kept the sitting position!

A fence of poles with a stout, arrow-proof gate surrounded the buildings of the trading post. Outside
the walls, in the Green Valley, were scattered the skin

lodges of trappers and their Indian mates, who waited for a share of trade with the passing throngs. These Indians, rich with trading, were bedecked with ribbons and beads. The women, mostly Shoshone, came from a tribe inclined to be friendly to strangers since the days when one of them, Sacajawea, the young Bird Woman, led the Lewis and Clark party westward. These friendly Indians came out to watch the Stephen wagons circle into place beside the stream. With them came a flock of children, their dark eyes bright with interest.

Bridger was in the fort when the wagons drew up. He was a small man, straightly built, and strong. The hardships of his life, with its constant exposure to all kinds of weather and danger, had so lined his face that he looked much older than his forty-odd years. He welcomed the families in to trade at his post. Sparks were soon flying in the blacksmith shop, where limping oxen and horses were shod, and iron wagon tires were replaced. Hans Sommer caressed the steel anvil with reverent hands.

Mrs. Stephen wasn't able to buy buckskin trousers for the boys, but she traded a red blanket to an Indian woman for two pairs of skin leggins. They were fringed at the sides, to the great satisfaction of Jim and Jerry.

Michael did some trading, too. He traded a pocket knife for a pair of beaded moccasins for Laura. But, though Laura's thanks let him know that she was happy with his gift, the joy of giving it to her was clouded when Michael learned that Silas Weeks had given a pair of moccasins to her, too! Why couldn't that meddlesome fellow have kept his moccasins to himself, or given them to some other girl, Michael thought. He sighed. If only he were a rich man now, instead of a penniless emigrant. He would show that Kentucky schoolmaster up—with his Indian moccasins! Michael didn't know that Laura laid Silas Weeks' gift away in a box, but kept his close at hand. He also had no idea that sometimes, at night, when her feet ached from the long day's walk, she slipped them into the little beaded moccasins Michael had given to her and felt wonderfully comforted. Only Laura knew that secret.

The travelers tasted a food new to them at Fort Bridger— dried service berries and choke cherries, ground to fine powder, mixed with water and baked in the sun. This was a favorite sweet of the Indian women from the Snake tribe.

"Look to see if those cakes have any grasshoppers and locusts in them," Devine said. When the boys laughed, he assured them that some Indians thought these, and other even less appetizing insects and bugs, very delicious food.

Flour was dear at Bridger, as it had been at Laramie, and sugar cost so much that Captain Stephen declared it was charged for by the grain. "We may be eating grasshoppers and bugs ourselves before we get to the Willamette Valley," the captain laughed. Jerry cringed. He didn't believe he could ever get that hungry.

Jim Bridger was leaving the fort early in the morning to guide a party of wealthy hunters from the East through the country, so Captain Stephen and Henri Devine sought him out that evening to tell him of the accidental shooting in the thicket and the threats of the Blackfeet. They took Jim and Jerry with them.

Bridger narrowed his eyes and shook his head when he had heard the story. Some careless whites, he said, were bringing trouble on others by dealing poorly with the natives. It would be getting harder and harder for covered wagon travelers as time went on. Every now and then an Indian was shot by a white man, in cold blood, for no cause at all, just as a boy would shoot a rabbit. The Indians might find it hard to believe that this accidental killing wasn't one of that kind. The Blackfeet people were a hard bunch to win over even under the best of circumstances. Now, due to the foolish actions of a few, it would be doubly difficult to keep the peace.

The famous scout told them that he was certain the Indians wouldn't be satisfied with one horse. They would want more.

"Make them a generous offer, and let them know that you consider the matter closed, if they come pesterin' you," he advised. "Don't let them see that they're worryin' you, and be sure to stick close together."

Then, in reply to young Jim's question as to whether Bridger had ever been shot by an Indian, the veteran of many close skirmishes smiled, drew away his shirt, and uncovered a deep scar on his shoulder where, years before, Dr. Marcus Whitman, missionary and physician, had cut an embedded arrowhead from Bridger's flesh.

"They've been after my ornery scalp fer a good many years, son," the fearless one said, "but Jim Bridger keeps a jump ahead of them. Never show an Indian you're afraid of him, boy. Remember that."

Young Jim pondered all that the venerable mountain man had said.

❖ ✦ ❖

Two days later, much refreshed, the Stephen Company left Fort Bridger. Myra had made friends with a little Indian girl and cried when she had to leave her behind. The small daughter of a trapper and a Snake woman stared with solemn dark eyes as the wagons jolted away. She had liked the little paleface girl; but she would never forget the marvelous white baby that she had held for a brief and blissful time, Myra's Annabelle.

❖ ✦ ❖

Early one afternoon, several days out from Fort Bridger, the leaders of the wagon train came across a message thrust into the split end of a stake beside the trail. These wayside messages were always important. Often they gave warnings that saved the readers from harm. This note read: "Water good here. Bad for two days ahead."

It was still two hours before the usual night-camping time, but camp was made at once to give the oxen the benefit of the good water. The wagons fell into place on a wide level near the good stream, and the bustle of making camp filled the air. When Jim had done his chores of carrying water and gathering wood, he turned his attention to the country around him. There was time for a little fun before supper. This was a fine place to practice being an Indian scout like Jim Bridger. The other boys were all busy, but he called Jerry, and they set out to scout around. It was a quiet place, far from everyone but their own people.

Jim led Jerry farther than he had intended, across the stream, out of sight of the wagons. But the noise of the camp, the lowing of cattle, the voices of the people were all about the boys. It didn't seem far. There was an elevation that tempted investigation. Beyond the hill was a thicket, a deep thicket that coaxed them on. Some good firewood there, and just the sort of place where Indians might hide, Jim thought with a pleased thrill. He fastened a bit of red cloth to a branch.

"The thing to do when you're scouting Indians!" he informed Jerry. Then he instructed the smaller boy to get down on his hands and knees to crawl through the underbrush.

"Like those Arapahoes did at Independence Rock," he whispered.

Delighted, Jerry did as Jim told him. This was a game to satisfy a boy's heart.

"Hist!" Jim whispered, shading his eyes and peering into the shadows of the thicket. "When I give the signal—"

He broke off with a sharp gasp. There was no make-believe in that gasp of horror. Jerry was instantly aware of danger that was very real. Jim did quick thinking in the breathless moment that followed. Without turning to Jerry, he whispered, "Real Indians ahead! Creep out of the thicket and run to camp! I'll follow! You can make it!"

"But, Jim," Jerry started to protest. The sharp backward thrust of Jim's foot spoke more forcefully than any words could have spoken.

"Quick! For your life … for mine—" Jim had risen to his feet and was walking right into the thicket, with his arms above his head!

Jerry obeyed. Something told him that their lives depended on his obedience to Jim's command and that failure to obey would be the end of them both. Flat on his face, he slid out of the thicket. Then, at the edge, he rose and ran for dear life toward camp. Up the hill to the crest he sped, down on the other side, through the stream—there were the wagons. Oh, it wasn't far! Surely Jim would make it as he had! There was Michael, going down to the stream. He was swinging a bucket and whistling. His song stopped abruptly when he caught sight of Jerry.

"Glory be!" exclaimed the Irishman. "What's wrong with the child?"

As he stared in puzzled alarm, Jerry stumbled and fell.

"Michael!" he screamed. "Indians, back there ... Jim, Jim—"

Michael raised his voice in a call for help. Men came running, rifles and pistols ready. Captain Stephen was first to reach Michael and Jerry. His eyes swept their frightened faces, and a sharp fear gripped him. Where was Jim?

Jerry began to sob at the sight of his uncle. Jim had not followed. He was back there, with the Indians.

"Maybe it's part of the game they were playin'," said Michael. He said this out of pity for the captain, who seemed to have grown old suddenly, adding the words that he knew were not true. "Sure, we'll find him, safe and sound."

But they did not find Jim. They found the place where the boys had stopped. Jerry pointed out the red cloth on the bush, but there was no trace of Jim, and no answer to their shouts, except the mocking answer of echoes. They found a place thirty yards beyond the thicket where horses had stood, but they were able to track the hoof prints only a short way, losing them soon in the rock and gravel. Now where? They stood helplessly, looking for some sign of hope. What course should they take? What direction? Hastily Devine divided them into searching parties to scour the country in all directions.

Captain Stephen's face was as white as a dead man's. Sweat stood on his forehead, and his eyes burned feverishly. The men turned away. They didn't like to look at him.

It was reasonable to assume that the Indians who had carried Jim away were Blackfeet, members of the raiding party at Black's Fork, and that they had taken this means of avenging their brother's killing. They must have been dogging the train for days, waiting for a chance to strike a blow. They hadn't killed Jim. They could have done so, easily. What did that mean? Were they going to hold him for ransom of horses? The men hoped that the captors would follow this course. Mean as it was, it was better than that they take him across the hundreds of miles to the Blackfoot territory in the foothills on the other side of the mountains, where he would be lost to his people forever. That sorrow, worse than death, had befallen other emigrant parents.

Devine laid his hands firmly on Captain Stephen's shoulders.

"Don't look on the dark side, Jim," he begged. "See here, your boy showed pluck and wit. He saw those Indians creeping up. He knew that if he and Jerry ran they both would be shot. By going toward them, he distracted their attention from the little fellow, so he could escape and give the alarm. Jim didn't get away, but those Indians won't kill him. They'll use him to buy horses from us. We'll keep the fires burning tonight to show them that we mean to stay here and bargain with them. Don't lose heart, Captain. We'll have Jim back before long!"

Captain Stephen's burning eyes stared blankly at the guide.

"His mother—" he began. Then he blurted out: "I've got to get off to search! Of course, you understand, men, you'll have to elect another captain. I can't leave this place until Jim is found, dead or alive. The wagons must go on ... but I must stay."

"But, man, your wife!" one of the men exclaimed.

Captain Stephen closed his eyes and passed a trembling hand over them.

"She must take care of Jerry!" he said brokenly. "She must go. I must stay."

Chapter 21

Captive in the Blackfoot Camp

When he caught sight of the braves creeping through the thicket toward him and Jerry, Jim's first impulse was to run. Terror laid hold of him, and for an instant his reasoning power was almost overcome. Then, clearly as a voice speaking to him, had come the thought: "If you run, they'll shoot. You got Jerry into this mess. You have to get him safely out."

Did the spirit of John Colter whisper now to the distracted boy? A mental picture came to him of that courageous man, exhausted from his long, cruel run, quickly turning to face his blood-thirsty pursuer, risking everything in a daring ruse. It was then as if all doubt were cleared away. Jim knew the course he should take. He sounded his warning to Jerry and gave his orders. Then he stood up, lifted his arms above his head, and walked straight toward the crouching

207

Indians. Colter's ruse worked again! Bewildered and astonished, the warriors crouched, staring at the boy who came toward them so fearlessly, and while they stared, motionless, Jerry made his escape, as Jim had hoped he would.

There was a point, however, that Jim had not worked out in his mind. That was how he would make his own escape. Every moment made that escape less possible. He couldn't hope to distract the Indians for long. There was no spear that he could snatch as Colter had, and there were four Indians to face. If only Jerry could give the alarm in time! If only some-one—his father, Michael, Dan—would come with a rifle before it was too late! But this was not to be. One of the Indians uttered a low exclamation and sprang forward. He had become aware of Jim's strategy. Jim's heart was up in his throat, beating like a hammer. He tried to run, tripped, and fell. He felt himself caught in an iron grip.

"Oh, Father! Michael! Come!" Jim didn't utter a sound, but his horrified being cried the words so strongly that he thought his tongue was shouting them. He thought he must be heard. A hand was clapped over his mouth, smothering him. He started to struggle. He kicked and fought with all his sturdy strength, and then, suddenly, everything was blotted out. He didn't feel the blow that deadened his senses.

✦ ✥ ✦

Later, when he woke to consciousness, Jim felt the after-effects of the blow, a thudding in his head and waves of stomach-sickness that robbed him of strength. He opened his eyes to darkness. He wondered what was making that awful pound, pound in his head and why he couldn't see. Becoming more alert, as his senses cleared, he felt himself held firmly and realized that he was being carried on a horse. Then it all came back to him: the Indians in the thicket, the struggle, the sudden darkness. His captors had him and were carrying him away. They had tied something over his face so he couldn't see. He leaned his head back against what he didn't know was the chest of a giant Blackfoot and cried silently. No one saw the tears that fell behind the cloth that bound his head—his own bandana handkerchief. He shut his teeth, recalling the words of Jim Bridger: "Never show an Indian you're afraid of him, boy!"

Jim vowed that he wouldn't let his captors know that he was afraid. They might torture him for the sport of hearing him beg for mercy, but he would not cry. A sickening worry haunted him. Had they overtaken and caught Jerry? He tried to remember everything that had happened before he had lost consciousness, but he couldn't be certain that Jerry had escaped. When they took the bandage from his head, at last, and he saw that Jerry was not in the group that surrounded him, such joyous relief swept him that he was able to meet the hard eyes of his captors quietly and fearlessly. He knew that he couldn't have stood it if Jerry had been there.

Jim was in the hidden camp of the Blackfeet raiding party that had caused such trouble at Black's Fork.

There were five men in the party. The boy sat, head swimming, jaws tightly clenched, looking from one face to another. The men were arguing. It was clear to Jim that they were disagreeing as to what should be done with him. In spite of all his effort at self-control, he found himself shrinking inwardly, remembering tales that he had heard of the treatment Indians sometimes gave captives, especially captives against whom they had a grudge. What would they do to him? It was about two hours before dusk when he and Jerry had started out on their game of scouting. Dusk was falling now. Only two hours away from his father's wagons, but how very, very far away he was! Frantically, Jim's mind worked with his problem. He knew that the Blackfeet would not stay long in that place. If they decided not to kill him they would take him with them early in the morning, and with each mile that they traveled the hope of being restored to his own people would grow dimmer. Better die than be lost to them forever, Jim told himself.

While the Indians argued, one, who had had little to say, put a pot of boiled meat among them, motioning for them to eat. They gave themselves up to their meal, eating as if they were famished. Then the silent one, either out of pity for Jim or admiration for his stoic calmness, dipped a small bowl in the greasy pot and handed it, half-filled with meat, to the boy. Jim ate the food, although he didn't taste it, so intent was his mind on the problem of escape. He was careful to wipe the greasy bowl out with his fingers. Persons sick with fear have no appetites. He would make his

Indian guards think that he enjoyed his meal. Maybe something would happen before dark.

Something did happen. The Blackfeet seemed to come, suddenly, to a decision. They were not going to kill their captive; at least, not that night. Jim knew this when he saw them preparing for sleep. A hopeful plan formed in his mind, but it was dashed to despair when an Indian went through his pockets, taking his knife away, and bound his wrists and ankles with stout strips of leather. Then someone threw a robe over him. Darkness settled on the hidden mountain camp. Jim lay with sleeping Indians all around him and stared with sick eyes up at the sky where stars had begun to blossom like white flowers in a great garden.

Suddenly, the boy became aware that someone was watching him. Instead of turning his head to encounter the watching eyes, he resorted to strategy. He yawned deeply, dropped his chin on his chest and closed his eyes. After an interval, he started to breathe deeply as sleepers do, pretending to sleep calmly when every nerve in his body was fairly throbbing. A low grunt behind him told him that his watcher was satisfied.

Jim's mind worked feverishly while he lay so quietly feigning rest. What could he do, bound hand and foot as he was? If he were loose he would take his chances trying to escape; to sneak out of the sleeping camp. Something stirred in his memory. Hadn't he heard of a captive's escape from a camp of sleeping Indians? Yes, he recalled clearly how Devine had told the children, not long ago, of how two Indian children, members of the Snake tribe, who had been stolen by an enemy tribe and carried far across the mountains, had made their safe escape at night while their captors slept. It had been done. It could be done again. If only his hands and feet were free!

A pain shot through the cramped muscles of his leg. Jim drew his knees up to relieve the strain. They came into contact with something hard. A stone! He moved his bound hands, cautiously, to examine the hard object. It was the bone bowl from which he had eaten his supper. He ran his finger along the brim. It was sharp ... sharp enough to cut! He began to tremble violently. A cold sweat broke out on his forehead, and the desire to cry like a baby shook him. He knew that this extreme nervousness was the natural result of the strain that he had been under. He knew that he would need almost superhuman strength for the strain that lay ahead. He had to shut his teeth and fight for calmness. The thought that with this unexpected help he might be able to cut the leather that bound his hands and feet was almost overpowering. He lay motionless for a while, fearing to betray by agitation his precious find. Then, working the bowl into a secure position between his up-drawn knees and his chest, he drew the cords on his wrists back and forth across the sharp rim of the bowl.

Not in five minutes, nor ten, nor twenty was it accomplished. It took perhaps an hour of painful, steady sawing—while perspiration ran from every pore and blood oozed from his lacerated wrists— before Jim's hands were free. Then, again, he lay motionless for a while, fighting for self-possession, praying for strength. With his hands free, it was not so difficult to cut the bonds that held his feet. There was one bad moment when Jim thought his movements had been discovered. An Indian cried out in his sleep. The frightened boy waited, every nerve on edge, but no one stirred. It came to him then with a thrill of hope that the sleepers were very sound asleep, since the cry had not disturbed them.

He lifted his head and looked around. The nearest Indian lay about two yards away. Jim could see the regular fall and rise of his breathing. Beyond that one lay another sleeper, relaxed and quiet. The way in that direction appeared clearest. The other members of the party were scattered about, rolled up in robes. Jim considered carefully. This was his one chance at escape. If he made a false move it was all over for him. Could he get past those two so near him without waking them? It seemed too much to hope for; still, those Snake children had accomplished the same thing. It had been done. It could be done!

Jim had spent much of his spare time since the attempted raid at Independence Rock sliding as the cunning Arapahoes must have slid, flat on the earth, never dreaming that he was to put the skill he was acquiring to a test, with his life depending on the outcome. He left his robe in a crumpled heap so it would appear that he still lay under it. Then, with a care born of desperation, he began his long slide across the ground. He lifted his head, now and then, to guide his course. There was nothing to shield him, and the clear starlight would have made him instantly visible if one of the sleepers had awakened.

An owl hooted. Jim pressed close to the earth, his heart thundering, and waited in a fever of suspense. Nothing happened. He slid on, inch by inch, moment by moment. "Our Father who art in heaven"; he prayed the one line of the old prayer over and over. He passed the nearest Indian. Another one now. Terror clutched him again when the sleeper sighed and turned in his direction. He lay motionless for what seemed an endless time, waiting for the disturbed Indian to rise or to sink back to rest, fearing every instant to feel the grasp of capturing hands as he had felt them that afternoon in the thicket. Again he took up his slow, painful crawl, inch by inch, moment by moment, until, at last, he lay quivering from head to foot, but safely outside of the sinister circle.

Jim was never able to estimate how far he crawled before he reached a place where he thought it safe to get up and run. Afterward it seemed unreal, night-marish, too terrible to have really happened to him. When he got stiffly to his feet and ran, the stars were fading and the darkness that precedes dawn was settling. He ran blindly, a small, desperate figure, not knowing, not caring what direction he took, seeking only a place of hiding, for he knew that with daylight the camp of Blackfeet would be astir and his escape would be discovered.

Down a steep hill he ran, into a ravine, stumbling, falling, bruising and cutting himself on rocks and brambles. Now and then he was forced to stop by sheer lack of breath, but fear of recapture drove him on. Every moment before daylight was precious. There would be time to rest later if he could escape.

So Jim drove and urged himself on until a faint flush showed in the sky. Then, weeping, in an hysterical mingling of relief and wretchedness, he crawled into a cleft in a rock hill. There, worn out, utterly exhausted, he fell asleep.

Chapter 22

Uncle Jack Robinson

As Jim was sleeping a sleep that was like the stupor of fever, deep and yet haunted by troubled dreams, a man passed within a few yards of his strange hiding place. The man moved with the graceful, noiseless tread of the trapper. No twig snapped under his moccasined feet, no grasses stirred at his passing. He seemed a silent part of the silent morning. He stooped and picked something from the ground. It was a narrow strip of buckskin. The eye of the ordinary man would have missed the small scrap, but nothing unusual in his wilderness world escaped the eye of the trapper. He examined the bit of buckskin and put it in his pocket. As he went on, slowly now, searching, he noted many things that told him, as plainly as speech, a story of flight—rocks fallen there that had been secure yesterday; branches broken here, where someone had grasped them in falling, and, finally, the faint outline of a bare human foot imprinted in soil moistened by a stream that trickled out of a rock hill.

This man, who came so early in the morning along the solitary way, was John Robinson, affectionately nicknamed "Uncle Jack Robinson," trapper and hunter, the first white settler in the mid-region of the Far West, who lived with his Indian mate not far from Fort Bridger, where he had built a cabin for his family in 1834. Uncle Jack Robinson turned when he had examined the footprint and went back to the spot where he had picked up the strip of buckskin. He wasn't long in discovering Jim. The ear of the trapper, attuned to the smallest voices of the wild, was keen to catch the foreign sound of human breathing. The man stood looking down at Jim, in a mingling of amazement and pity.

Uncle Jack Robinson had come across many unusual things in these early morning excursions of his, some of them pleasant, and some of them sad. He had come, often, upon nests where baby bears cuddled like sleepy puppies and lifted curious heads to blink at him as he went by. More than once, he also had stepped over the dead body of a painted brave who lay where his vanquishers had left him, the lacerated flesh of his head showing red and raw where a scalping knife had been busy. But never before had he happened upon such an utterly astonishing thing as this—a young boy, asleep in a rock cave, miles from human habitation, tear-streaked cheeks telling a

tale of grief and terror, and blood-caked, swollen feet speaking of long, hard travel.

The trapper stood for a while staring down at Jim. An emigrant boy, he told himself. But how had he come to this hidden place, so far from the wagon route? How had he found his way here, unless he had been driven or carried by Indians? Uncle Jack Robinson stepped to one side and called gently to Jim to waken him. He knew that it would startle the boy to wake and find a stranger standing over him—a stranger whose shoulder length hair and bronzed skin made him look more like an Indian than an American trapper.

He called repeatedly. It was hard for the exhausted boy to rouse. When Jim opened his eyes and sat up, bewildered, it was to hear a pleasant, kindly voice, speaking reassuringly, "Don't be afeered, sonny. I'm a friend to one like yoreself."

Looking around, he met the smiling eyes of Uncle Jack Robinson. He stared at the man in a dazed manner, and he couldn't believe until he had touched him and felt the warm grasp of his hands that this was not part of a dream. When he knew that the man was real and a friend, Jim clung to his hands and cried and laughed with relief. He felt that his troubles were over now. But the trapper, when he had heard of the Blackfeet, looked serious and concerned.

"They'll be along soon, lookin' fer you," he said. "They'll be able to trail you same as I did." He pondered for a moment. "I'm alone out here—been huntin' fer a couple of days. Can't hide you in my tent. It's pitched over yonder about two miles." His lean face took on a determined expression. "There's only one thing to do," he said. "We've got to git out of here. Come on!"

Jim tried to walk, but his swollen feet refused to hold him. He tottered and leaned back against the rock. Without a word, Uncle Jack Robinson lifted him, hoisted the heavy boy to his back, and started off. Then, with an exclamation, he set Jim down, took the sharp knife from his belt, and cut the fringe from the boy's leggins.

"Whar did ya git them leggins?" he asked.

"At Fort Bridger," Jim replied. "My mother bought them from an Indian woman."

Uncle Jack laughed. "Lucky fer you that Injun wom'n warn't a good sewer!" he said. "I might not of found you if I hadn't seen that thar bit of fringe. But we won't take any chances now on leavin' a trail of fringe fer the Injuns to foller."

The trapper wasn't a large man, nor was he powerfully built, but he carried Jim with the ease of one whose muscles were perfectly trained, and when he reached his camp he was neither winded nor worn.

A roll of blankets and a heap of ashes told where the man of the wilderness had made his camp for the night. Not far away, a splendid mare was tethered. She neighed a welcome to her master. Uncle Jack put Jim down on the blankets and poured a cup of water for him. Then, as gently as a woman would have, he bathed the cut and swollen feet, and bound them with strips torn from his blanket. He shook his head over those feet.

"Won't be able to do much foot-travelin' fer some time, sonny!" he said. "But like as not they'll be so glad t' git you back that they'll let you ride in the wagon."

"Do you think we'll be able to find them?" Jim asked anxiously.

"Shore we will," said the hunter, "if the Injuns don't git us, an' I don't reckon they will! Never seed an Injun yit that didn't have a heap of respect fer my ol' Betsy, here!" He patted his rifle. "An' as fer findin' yore folks, that'll be easy with Molly's help. Molly—she's my mare, and one of the best pals a man ever had."

The kindly trapper made it all seem very simple, a matter of a few hours' pleasant travel, for he could see that Jim had been tried to the breaking point; but the ride that they had to make was a grueling experience. To avoid running into the Blackfeet, his guide swung far off the customary route and urged his mare with her extra burden through an unbroken and all but unbreakable country. They traveled where it seemed foolhardy to attempt to pass. Always the mountain man walked, and several times Jim had to slip from the mare's back and make his way painfully on his swollen feet. He was half-fainting from fatigue when they reached the wagon trail. The going was easy then, and in the hope of seeing his dear ones again, Jim's spirits soared. He told Uncle Jack Robinson that he thought he could run ahead of Molly, but the wise friend smiled and shook his head.

"Best let Molly do the walkin'," he said. "Her hoofs are toughest an' she has four of them."

As the weary day wore on, Jim's fatigue grew overpowering, and to keep him awake Uncle Jack Robinson kept urging him to watch the road.

"Look here boy, do ya recollec' this here place?" he would ask, and Jim would open his tired eyes and scan the wagon trail helplessly. There was not a familiar landmark. But he had told Uncle Jack of the message held in the split stake by the side of the trail near where they had made their encampment. The trapper was watching for that signpost. Late in the afternoon he saw it.

"Water good here," he read; "bad for two days ahead."

Jim was too spent to notice the sign. His guide turned Molly off the wagon road and led her to the top of an incline. There, below, in camp formation, were the Stephen wagons, waiting while the men scoured the country for the boy whom even the most hopeful had given up hope of ever seeing again.

Uncle Jack Robinson fired his old Betsy into the air. Instantly, the camp was in an uproar. People came running from all directions toward the man, boy, and horse who appeared to have risen out of the earth. When Jim slid from Molly's tired back, he fell into his mother's arms.

Uncle Jack Robinson had to tell the story of the escape from the Blackfeet, for Jim was beyond talking. His sore feet dressed by Dr. Dean, he was soon sound asleep in the Home Wagon. Jerry took up his station there, and when the other boys came tiptoeing around, eager for a word with Jim, the little watchman warned them away.

"He's still asleep," he whispered, "an' it looks like he's going to sleep for some time."

Jim's mother and father knew that night when they looked down on their safely sleeping boy that they were the happiest people in the world.

"To think that I cried about leaving a chest behind, Jim! A wooden chest!" Beth Stephen whispered. Her eyes were filled with tears now, but they were happy tears.

Uncle Jack Robinson slept in the wagon camp that night and was off on Molly early in the morning, long before Jim was awake. He left a message for Jim: "Tell the youngun' that if I meet up with the Blackfeet, I'll give 'em his respec's. And ya might let him know that if ever he wants to go into the trappin' business, he kin sign up with his Uncle Jack Robinson. He's the pluckiest boy I ever did see!"

Chapter 23

Fort Hall

Up the wagons toiled, eight thousand feet into the air, to the top of the ridge that divided the Green and Bear Rivers. Off in the distance the travelers could see the lovely Three Tetons, graceful peaks that rose abruptly from the storied Jackson's Hole, to a height of over ten thousand feet. Down into the beautiful Valley of the Bear they rolled, down into what the children thought was gloryland.

It was really very closely akin to gloryland—one of the parks of the Rockies. Here were grass for the hungry livestock, lots of it; pure drinking water; wildflowers for the children to gather, as pretty, almost, as the wildflowers at home; and in the crystal-clear streams were great, speckled trout. The men caught strings of them for the women to fry to delicious brownness. They scooped them up with nets made of canvas, for the trout were so well fed on gnats and insects that they wouldn't touch bait.

In their delight over this pleasant country, the travelers could almost forget the stinging gnats that rose in swarms from the thick grass and the Snake Indians that crowded around the wagons in curiosity, pulling back the canvas to peer in, even trying to lift the lids from the pots to see what the women were cooking. The children wished that they might stay right there for days, but, "Travel! Travel! Travel!" was a command forever ringing in the ears of the emigrants. They said good-bye to the country that had held so much true enjoyment for them, the country that is now part of the state of Wyoming. The Stephen Company continued their way on into what is now Idaho, named so after an expression of the Shoshone Indians "Ee-dah-how!" meaning, "Look, the sun is coming down the mountains!"

At Soda Springs, the little pioneers drank quarts of soda water, sharp and pleasant in flavor, and marveled at a great spout of hot water that shot into the air at regular intervals called Steamboat Spring. Here Michael's Beauty, poking around, got his curious nose burned. His outraged brays started all the mules in camp to braying. And beyond Soda Springs, on the sandy bank of Snake River, was Fort Hall. This place was sought out by overland travelers with the eagerness with which they had looked forward to the Platte, Fort Laramie, and that ridge in the South Pass whence the trail led down onto truly Western land.

The outer walls of Fort Hall were solidly built of sun-dried brick. The fort had two bastions that were studded with loopholes, where rifles could be thrust to discourage the too-close approach of troublemakers.

"Wonder if they have to use those rifle-holes often," Jim asked.

The truth was that the Hudson's Bay Company, owner of Fort Hall since 1837, when it was purchased from its builder, Nathaniel Wyeth, rarely had to use rifles against the Indians. The Native Americans west of the Rockies, in the Oregon Country, where Hudson's Bay forts were established, gave little trouble in the first years of covered-wagon travel. They had learned to trust and respect the Hudson's Bay men.

Fort Hall was a busy place. It was a general refitting and overhauling station for wagons, and for some emigrants it was the place of a sudden complete change of plans. Here many, who had thus far had Oregon in mind, decided to take the trail that branched off the Raft River, three days out from Fort Hall, and led across the Humboldt Desert and through the Sierras, into California; while others, who had been thinking of California, were here persuaded to follow the Oregon Trail on down the Snake, through the Blue Mountains, and finally down the Columbia to the

Willamette River. Fortunes and futures were changed overnight at old Fort Hall.

Here the Stephen Company saw many abandoned wagons, for, in the early days of the trail, it was thought that no Oregon-bound wagon dared venture far beyond the fort. True, the missionary, Dr. Whitman, had taken wheels through in 1836, as far as Fort Boise, two hundred miles to the west, but his pioneering wagon had been cut down, gradually, until it was no more than a two-wheeled cart when it reached the fort.

"It's sheer madness to try to take those heavy wagons through country where there's only a foot trail!" So said everyone at Fort Hall.

Indians, trappers, and traders who found the route difficult even for sure-footed horses, added scornful comments. "Wagons? Are you crazy? How will you get wagons down sheer cliffs? How'll you get them over trails where there's hardly room for a horse? And what of the Blue Mountains beyond the Snake canyons?"

Despite these warnings, in 1843 wagons had wheeled doggedly past Fort Hall, as they had pressed on through the obstacles of the prairies, plains, deserts, rivers, and mountains. But when the Stephen wagons came in 1844, there was still much head shaking over taking prairie schooners through the district of the Snake. There were terrible stories of wagons and animals toppling from cliffs, of human lives lost, of bodies crippled, of minds lost through suffering. Those stories turned many toward California.

Captain Stephen heard the warnings with a troubled heart. Did he dare to expose these lives in his care to such danger? Would it be better to abandon the wagons and take only such things that could be carried with pack-horses and mules? The Stephen men held an anxious meeting there at the fort and decided in favor of wagons. Wheels had been taken through, and what others had done they could do, they decided. Wagons had been unloaded and lowered down canyon walls, sometimes with ropes made from the braided hides of oxen, poor beasts that, worn out by the long miles of hauling, had been killed to give this last service to their masters. And men had cut roads, time and time again, for the wagons and oxen to travel. They would take the wagons. It could be done.

This decision made, the men fell to work, making ready for the trials that faced them. Prairie schooners were shortened. Some of them, badly worn, were cut in two and transformed into light carts. And every load was lightened again.

Snake Indians watched the preparations with great interest. They sorted over the outcast things, grunting with disgust at some and with satisfaction over others. Mrs. Dean traded a frock coat and a dress hat of the doctor's to an Indian brave for some dried salmon. The big fellow, dressed only in a breech clout and moccasins, put on the hat and coat and paraded around proudly, to the great envy of all his male companions and the ardent admiration of their women.

Jerry and Jim and Myra, chewing the tough, fat skin of the salmon, watched the vain antics of the dressed-up Indian with delight. He had seemed well dressed before, in nothing much more than his bare skin. Now he was quite amusing. The children wished that there were more clothes to trade for dried salmon. They had never tasted anything so good.

"Be careful of the Islands ford!" Fort Hall officials warned as the Stephen wagons pulled away. "Nearly every company leaves a grave at that crossing, if they're lucky enough to fish the corpse out of the water."

So, with hope and dread battling in their hearts, the Stephen wagon train turned out from Fort Hall. The night before they left, while Myra was sound asleep, Dr. Dean took Annabelle's cradle out of the wagon. The time had come when it must go. Carefully, he laid it down and covered it. Myra would be spared the

grief of seeing her trea-
sure left behind. But
Michael had seen.

"Now, that's
too bad!" he
said to himself.
"Annabelle will
be missin' her
bed. Goodness
me, she'll never
be able to sleep at
all without it."

The next morn-
ing, when the wag-
ons took up the
march, Michael's
Beauty, already laden
with a pack almost as big as himself, bore a new burden—a small mahogany cradle rode triumphantly
on top of his pack.

Chapter 24

Mad River

"Mad River"—so the explorers had called the Snake. The name was fitting, for the river was mad in places, and it had driven men mad. But its course, though marked by human suffering, was also brightened by the glory of human bravery.

Those gallant path-breakers, the Astorians, led by Wilson Price Hunt, seeking a way overland from the Missouri to the Columbia River in 1811, caught in the Snake canyons, their way blocked by giant rocks, had known days of near-madness in this terrible region. They were the first white party to travel this route where the Oregon Trail was later to run. Wandering, lost, half-crazed from thirst before they found a way through to the Columbia, the Astorians left their own trail of glory in the Snake regions. And other brilliant trails were there before the covered wagons came with their brave defiance of the "Mad River."

The children heard, often now, a sound new to them, a truly Western sound—the mysterious, booming "voice of many waters," for the Snake was a river of giant falls. Down there, in the canyons, far below where the covered wagons crawled along a narrow trail, great mountains of water swept and crashed over the rocks.

Sometimes, at night, Jerry awakened and cringed, hearing that thundering boom, boom, boom. He had never known a river with a voice like that, so wild, so big. But this was a western river, Uncle Jim said, with an echo of the ocean in its voice. It was a branch of the Columbia, the great river of Oregon.

The Indian camps, too, were different now from any the travelers had seen. These Snake River natives were all fishermen, who stood all day on the wet rocks and thrust long, shining spears into the foam where big silver salmon fought their way. Those thrusting lances were very sure. The arms that thrust them had had much practice. Long lines of stiff red slabs, the drying flesh of the western fish, were strung about every camp.

→ ‡ ←

August was drawing to a close when the tattered wagons of the Stephen Company came down the steep incline to the first ford of the Snake, known as the Islands ford. The warning heard at Fort Hall was recalled now: "Nearly every company leaves a grave at the Islands crossing, if they're lucky enough to fish the corpse out of the water."

Mrs. Dean sat with her arm around Myra as they rested on the river shore. She looked at the wide, swift river. Her arm tightened around the child, and her lips whispered a prayer. With the same thoughts troubling her mind, Mrs. Stephen watched Jim and Jerry, who stood with a group of excited boys looking at the river. Questions that she tried to hush kept repeating themselves. Whose would it be? Whose grave would their company leave at the Islands ford? Ah, please,

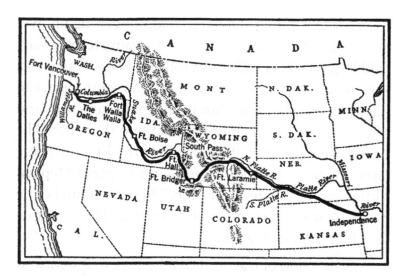

God, not any grave! So did all the women pray as they helped the men make ready for the crossing.

The drivers were yoking the strongest oxen so they could lead the wagons. Men were getting the best horses saddled and herding the cattle into line. The cattle eyed the water nervously, sensing a struggle ahead.

Here, where the crossing was to be made, were two islands. Because of the islands, this point was the safest fording place, for the solid earth, rising from the water, gave the animals and drivers a chance to rest and recover their breath.

Henri Devine gave orders that were carried from man to man. "Five wagons and their teams chained together in a strong line," he ordered, "with the drivers on the downstream side to guide the oxen."

Devine went on ahead to test the crossing. He rode slowly, letting his trained horse pick his way, noting carefully the strength and sweep of the current. The water rose, lapping the horse's sides, washing up over his back, while the brave animal swam steadily, ears laid back, nostrils wide, eyes rolling. The air rang with cheers when the horse struggled up out of the water to the safety of the first island. The guide signaled, and the first string of wagons wheeled into the water. The Stephen wagon was at the head of the line, carrying Mrs. Stephen, Jim, and Jerry, with Captain Stephen riding on the downstream side. They pulled up beside Devine on the first island in triumph. The first step had been accomplished.

One section of wagons after another followed, and the spare horses and oxen were driven into the water by the herders, shepherd dogs swimming alongside, their faithful eyes on their charges. "Swimming the cattle" was fun for the adventurous young men, but it called for care and skill.

A wild flood swept between the two islands.

Facing that churning water, women and children paled and questioned one another with frightened eyes that tried to smile.

Devine plunged into the water, and again his horse, nervous and trembling from the swim, staggered up out of the channel. The second island had been reached! He raised his hand in signal and the wagons followed. The water swept up, soaking the canvas covers, wetting the wagon contents, but no one noticed that. Every mind was set on victory over the river. One after the other the wagon lines pulled up onto the island. The second step had been achieved! A third remained.

When he had seen the first wagons make the second island in safety, Devine rode into the last sweep of water toward the landing place on the north shore of the Snake. The distance from the island to the north shore was a full two thousand six hundred feet. The swift current swept over a bar, and the floor of the last channel was broken by holes.

"Don't follow until I give the signal," the guide had warned.

Watching the water lash up on the horse and rider, and seeing the animal fight against the current, children began to cry. Myra gave way to terror and sobbed aloud, "I don't want to go! Oh, I don't want to go!"

Jerry closed his eyes. Best not look at this water, he reasoned. Best try to pretend that it wasn't there. It was hard to pretend, though, and he found that he couldn't keep his eyes closed. The oxen were tossing their heads and rolling their eyes. They were afraid, too!

Devine didn't signal, at once, for the wagons to follow. He stood for a while beside his horse, looking at the water through which they had just battled. Captain Stephen understood. It meant that the guide had found the crossing very difficult. He sent this word of caution along the line. Finally, the awaited order came.

"Come along!" Devine signaled.

The Stephen oxen plunged into the water. A hush had fallen on the island. Even the bellowing cattle were stilled.

Through the waiting silence, a boy's voice rang out. "Hi, there, Jim and Jerry! Safe across!"

It was little Tom Foster, whose father's wagon headed the second string. He had climbed up onto a box in the front of the wagon. That glad shout gave heart to the hearers and a ripple of laughter followed. Wet eyes smiled again, and tense nerves relaxed.

"See, we are getting there all right, boys!"

Mrs. Stephen said, "It won't be much longer now."

The wagons battled safely through the water that seemed to roar in anger at this intrusion and came up on the rocky north shore, victorious.

"We're over! We're over!" shouted Jerry, clambering from the dripping wagon, and Myra, who had been just behind Jim and Jerry, jumped down to join Jerry on the shore. There was laughter and shouting to cheer those still in the water's grasp. But suddenly, the cheering stopped, and laughing lips turned ashen. Something had happened to the lead team of the Foster wagon. The chain had broken and the oxen were floundering. Men, accustomed now to river crossings, worked with skillful speed. Ropes were thrown about the floundering oxen, and they were pulled back into line.

"Hold tight! Hold tight!" Tom Foster shouted hoarsely. His voice was lost in the tumult. He was shouting to little Tom, who was clinging to the shaking wagon. Even as the oxen were pulled back into line, the boy slipped from the wagon and went down into the water, out of sight. A red bandana handkerchief flashed in the white foam below the island where the water was deep and swift.

"He's gone!"

But, no! There was a dark head in the water between the oxen and the wagon, and Tom bobbed up, unharmed, blowing water from his mouth, laughing! He was holding on to the ox's tail!

＊ ‡ ＊

Later, when the wagons rested safely on shore, when fires were crackling cheerily, and there was time to rest and talk, Tom told the story of his close escape.

"When I fell I landed right on old Buck's back," he said. "I tried to stick there, but it was too slippery and I slid off. I guess I touched the bottom of the river, just about. I could feel the current pullin' me away, and I grabbed for somethin' to take hold of. Then old Buck, he sort of bent down so's I could get hold of his tail. Just sort of put his tail right in my hands. It was easy then."

Nothing could shake Tom's belief that his father's ox had come to his help intentionally. The children didn't question the matter, and they scurried around to gather every green morsel that they could find for old Buck, the remarkable animal that had cheated the "Mad River" of its prey.

＊ ‡ ＊

September found the wagons toiling through that part of the Snake Valley known as the sage deserts of the mountains, the hardest country they had yet

encountered. Some days, the trail led along a high pla-
teau, where all was a desolation of sage and cactus.
Some days, the children had to walk single file, keeping
close to a wall of rock that towered, surely, to heaven,
Myra thought. God's throne, she had it figured out,
was up there on the tip-most top. Could He see them
from way up there? Below, where the edge of the road
dropped away into space, the river raced through its
canyons, and it was tormenting to know, when their
throats were parched with thirst, that down there was
water, clear and cold, they couldn't reach.

Mirages added their taunt to the difficult miles.
Sun-wearied eyes, looking over the endless miles of
sage and dust, saw lovely lakes, fringed by green trees,
off in the distance. It was hard for the children to
believe that the lakes and trees weren't there at all, that
they were only eerie reflections, desert mirages, opti-
cal illusions. Cruel tricks, they were, that sometimes
lured overland travelers far into alkali wastes, where
weird lava formations, glaring white in the blazing
sun, stood like mocking sentinels of a ghostly country, and where there wasn't a drop of water in all the
terrible miles. There was a story told by Indians and
trappers of a river out there in the lava wastes; Lost
River, it was called, where thirsty men, after traveling miles through blistering sand, found only a grim
taunt—a dry river bed. There were skeletons to mark
the place, the Indians and trappers said.

At times, Jerry was certain that their caravan was
lost, wandering hopelessly. "Jim, do you s'pose we'll
ever get to Oregon?" he asked; and Jim, stoutly assur-

ing him that they weren't lost, that they were following a trail that had led others safely, felt only half-convinced, himself, that this was true. Those men at Fort Hall hadn't lied about this part of the trail. How had those wagons of the year before gone through, with no wagon road, at all, to guide them? In the Blue Mountains, the Stephen wagons bumped for miles over stumps of trees that the trailblazers of 1843 had cut to make a passage.

The month of Indian summer was drawing to a close when the groaning wagons and limping walkers came down the western slopes of the Blue Mountains. Everyone walked now, and the going on weary feet was slow. Cows replaced worn-out oxen on some of the wagons. Two-wheeled carts were numerous, and Hans Sommer's wagon was only a handcart in which he wheeled the precious remnants of his blacksmith shop. Chief Wolf's Brother's horses bent their proud heads beneath loads as heavy as they could bear. Some of the cattle lay down at every stop, their ribs all but sticking through their hides. Shepherd dogs wore bindings of buckskin on their raw feet.

Out of the Blue Mountains the weary walkers came, and their tired hearts lightened when they saw herds of sleek Cayuse ponies feeding on the rich plains of the Umatilla River. The skin tepees of the Cayuse Indians spoke to the homeless ones of home and rest, and the sharp tang of autumn fires was sweet to their nostrils.

Indian children, Cayuse and Nez Percés (French for "people of the rocks" and "pierced noses," respectively), played in the green meadows among the spotted ponies.

They stopped their romping to stare at the lumbering, dusty wagons and the tattered palefaces that wound along that trail, so new to the Indian country.

These native folk of the river country called the wagons "horse canoes." Many of these people asked, "Are there any people left in the white man's land?" They had never seen so many strangers.

The Stephen Company children looked hungrily at something the little Indians chewed with great relish, dried blue lupine and camas root. It looked good!

Whitman Mission, on the bank of the Walla Walla River, named Waiilatpu ("place of rye grass") by the Cayuse, cheered the covered-wagon travelers. Here was a pioneer home, the first they had seen since they left their own. Mrs. Whitman, Narcissa, the first pioneer woman to travel the Oregon Trail, won the admiration of all the Stephen women. She had come over that awful way in 1836. She knew all about it! How pretty she looked in her clean, starched dress, and how kindly she greeted them in her beautiful, cultured voice! She laid her hand on Myra's curly head, and her bright face shadowed as she looked down at the little girl. They understood that look of sadness when they learned that the Whitmans' only child, a little girl, had been drowned in the river nearby. The boys looked on Dr. Whitman as a hero, not because he had come from his home far in the East to live among the Western people and teach them of God, but because he was the man who had cut the arrowhead from Jim Bridger's shoulder!

Down into the Columbia Valley the emigrants now took their way. On clear days they had sight of Mt. Hood, the beacon mount of Oregon, looming up awesome and beautiful, as if it had stood since the creation of the world and would stand forever. Its snowy head shown like silver against the marvelous azure of the Oregon sky. At last they had their first glimpse of the Columbia, broad blue river of promise. They had cheered and sung at the sight of the muddy Platte. They could only stand voiceless now, tears streaming down their cheeks. Near Fort Walla Walla, a Hudson's Bay post on the Columbia, they made their last wagon encampment. They were not yet at journey's end, but the wheeled caravan would be broken at this spot. The Stephen Company would have to proceed to its final destination without the help of wagons.

Chapter 25

Down the Columbia with the Voyagers

The Columbia River was now the last great obstacle between the travelers and their chosen goal—the Willamette Valley. There was no wagon road through the snowy Cascade Mountain Range, so it was necessary for the overlanders to become sailors and travel down the Columbia River that had cut a channel through the mountains. This was travel new to them. They had forded dozens of rivers, but they must ride down this one on flat boats, rafts, and canoes for a week, perhaps longer. It would be no holiday excursion with the water swollen by fall rains and whipped by rugged October winds.

The Stephen Company stayed encamped near Fort Walla Walla for ten days, while the men worked from dawn until dusk building flat boats and rafts from the timber that was washed in by the waves. The boats must be strong enough to withstand heavy buffeting. There were rapids in the Columbia down which craft were swept with the speed of arrows; there were shallows, as much to be feared as rapids, where a boat might come to grief on hidden rocks; there were narrows, where the water boiled rather than flowed, and where overhanging cliffs seemed almost to meet.

The children looked forward to sailing with keen pleasure. It would be fun to ride on the clean, dustless water after months of trudging over stones and dirt. While they waited for the building of the boats, they played with the Indian children—Walla Walla, Cayuse, and Nez Percés. These Native American children shared with them the sweet camas and lupine root, and a parsnip-like vegetable that the little Indians called "yampa."

The older people could not share the children's joy, facing that river trip. They knew the western river's power. They had heard of how emigrants, members of the Applegate Company, riding down the Columbia on open skiffs, had met tragedy the previous year in the narrows. Only a few yards from shore one of the skiffs had been swept over, and three of the party, Alexander McLellan, an old soldier, and two young Applegate boys, Warren and Edward, had been drowned.

Captain Stephen was relieved to get two French-Canadian boatmen—*voyageurs* (French for "travelers"), employees of the Hudson's Bay Company—to pilot his leading craft and lead the way for the others.

The voyageurs were among the most expert boatmen in the West. They were a rollicking lot, not tall men, for there was no room for long legs in the canoes in which they skimmed the waters, but lithe and graceful, and powerfully developed in the arms and shoulders. They were born for their work of piloting craft through all kinds of water, and of making long portages, carrying canoes and packs overland, where it was impossible to go by water. They loved their work and laughed at danger. They sang their hardy songs where the water was wildest, shooting through the strongest currents, the roughest eddies, while keeping time with swinging paddles to the tunes they sang.

Jerry and Jim watched them in speechless admiration. There was an air of romance, of adventure, about these men that was fascinating.

One favorite melody of the singing boatmen wove itself into the memories of the boys. The words were French, but the boys learned the English words later, and the refrain was unforgettable:

Malbrouck has gone a-fighting—
Mironton, mironton, mirontaine!
Malbrouck has gone a-fighting—
Will he return again?

The ballad told how Malbrouck's lady climbed her watchtower to look for his return, which, alas, was never to be. Instead of her awaited lord, a page came to tell her of the gallant Malbrouck's death on the battlefield and his glorious burial. And thus the page closed his faithful message very logically:

I say no more, my lady—
Mironton, mironton, mirontaine!
Say no more, my lady,
For naught more doth remain.

Ever after, this ballad would remind the children of their thrilling ride down the Columbia in an open boat. The song would awaken memories of the voyageur at its prow, his head bound with a bright kerchief and his hair—worn long as a protection against gnats and mosquitoes—flying in the wind. It was also to recall, all their lives long, the tingling dash of cold spray on their cheeks, the strange pulse of the waves beneath them, as if a giant heart beat down there in the water. They would never forget the sharp lash of wind that made their blood race, the boom of falls, the swift slide down a hill of water—the joy, the terror of their river voyage.

The Dalles Indians, standing on the Columbia banks like bronze statues, watched, fishing spears held suspended in their hands, as the flat boats swept past, laden with paleface women and children and household goods.

"Bostons," these Indians of the Far West called the emigrants, because the first Americans on the coast had come by way of ship from Boston. The use of the name had spread.

"They have no fear, these Bostons!" the natives said with awe and admiration, adding in more somber tones, "Will they never stop coming?"

Jerry and Jim shouted and waved their hands at the watching Indians, and Myra held Annabelle high for them to see. So they rode down toward Fort

Vancouver, human freight borne on the heaving surface of the Columbia.

The wagons and most of the Stephen livestock were left at Fort Walla Walla to be cared for through the winter, and the cattle were branded with the "H.B.C." of the Hudson's Bay Company. Beauty was among the few animals that had the strength to travel straight through to the end, following an Indian trail along the shore. Chief Wolf's Brother's gift horses, too, kept to the trail with their heavy packs.

"Beauty is too stubborn to give up," Michael laughed. But Myra wouldn't listen to that.

"It's because he wants to carry Annabelle's cradle to our new home!" she declared. "He knows she'll want to sleep in it right away."

In places, where the water was too dangerous for them to risk, as at The Dalles, where the boats had to "shoot the rapids" and pass through a narrow, crooked channel called "the Devil's Gullet," the women and children walked along the Indian trail. The children picked haws, the scarlet berries of hawthorn and wild rose, and ate them as hungrily as wild birds eat. These berries were a sorry substitute for the fresh fruit they had not tasted for months.

The Indians eyed them with placid curiosity. These natives were accustomed to people from the East. Dr. John McLoughlin, the *Hyas Tyee* ("Great Chief"), and "King George's men," the British Hudson's Bay Company employees, had been long in their midst.

At night, camp was made among the towering rocks that walled the river. Wood was plentiful in this country of giant evergreens, larch and fir, and cedar. The night fires threw red reflections on the dark water. The screams of eagles that hovered near the water to feed on the remains of salmon echoed among the crags. The ghostly hoots of night owls and the never-ceasing howls of wolves filled the darkness with wild clamor, but the children didn't hear. They slept the sleep of utter weariness in their rude beds on the river shore. They huddled close under worn coverings, for the October nights were cold, and their blood was thinned by lack of nourishing food. The dreams of the little pioneers now were mostly about food. All of the children had lost a great deal of weight. They needed food, and plenty of it.

Beth Stephen noticed with pain that Jerry's face, round and rosy at the beginning of their travel, was sunken now, and too thin for a child. His eyes seemed too large for his face; but, the thought cheered her, the Willamette Valley was not far away now. When they had been out on the prairies she had reassured the boys and herself with the reminder: "Every day is nearer than yesterday." She could say now: "Only a few days more."

Chapter 26

Dr. John McLoughlin and Fort Vancouver

"Jerry! Wake up!"

Jim took his little cousin by the shoulder and shook him. Jerry sighed a long, shuddering sigh. Half waking, he thought that the open flat boat on which they had traveled all night had struck heavy swells and was pitching about. His eyes opened slowly. An annoyed frown creased his brows. "What now?" asked Jerry. "A fellow can't buy a moment's peace any more!"

"Say, you're not awake yet, Jerry!" he cried. "Look! We're here!"

"Ummm ... where?"

"Fort Vancouver! Open your eyes! Look, Jerry, there's the fort up there on the flat. Wow, it must be a big place!"

Jerry raised himself on his elbow and looked where Jim's outstretched arm pointed. A cloud of fog was lifting from the river, and through its misty veil the boys could make out what appeared to be a town built on a wide, green slope that ran up from the river. Below, at a dock, two schooners flying British flags rocked gently on the waves. To the boys, inland bred and unused to water craft, the schooners looked enormous.

Jerry rubbed his eyes and looked again. Their flat boat was drawn up on the sandy shore, and a camp

had been
made out of reach
of the river tide; a real
tide from the not far distant Pacific Ocean. Fires were
crackling and excited voices were raised in talk and
laughter. The women were busy getting breakfast.
Breakfast lately had been nothing to get excited about;
but this morning there was a promising fragrance in
the air. It brought Jerry back to Auntie Kay's kitchen.
He sniffed.

"What's that I smell?" Jerry demanded.

Jim laughed again. "How do I know what you
smell? Get up, lazybones, and see for yourself."

He sprang ashore and ran toward the camp. "Better
hurry!" he called. "It won't last long!"

Jerry threw back the covers, and a cloud of steam
escaped into the chill air. The covers were soaking. It

had rained furiously during the night, and he had slept soundly in a puddle. He shivered now, his teeth chattering. The morning air bit to his bones, but he forgot discomfort in the delight of that wonderful smell that was wafting out from the campfires. He didn't have to dress. Practically all the clothing he had to his name was on his body. He jumped from the boat and ran after Jim to their campfire.

Aunt Beth smiled at him, and, surprised, he noticed that her cheeks, so pale lately, were pink and that her eyes were shining and excited. Something very glad leaped in Jerry's heart. Aunt Beth lifted the lid from a skillet and disclosed to the little boy's astonished eyes a mound of browned potatoes. Then she lifted another lid, and there was a piece of boiled salmon, swimming in fat juice. There were a loaf of bread and a pat of yellow butter and a big pot of steaming tea. There were a jug of rich milk and a dish of sugar. He could only stare. Jim clapped his hands. He had been waiting to see that look of blank bewilderment on Jerry's face.

"Isn't it wonderful, Jerry!" Aunt Beth said. "It's a gift to our company from Dr. McLoughlin, at the fort."

Jerry didn't know who Dr. McLoughlin was, but he put him down then and there as one of the world's grandest men. All their lives the children remembered that breakfast on the bank of the Columbia, in the shadow of Fort Vancouver. An air of holiday hung over the camp that day. Warmed and comforted by a delicious meal that had been given in friendship, the emigrants relaxed and "put their cares behind them."

There was much happy planning and laughter, and occasionally there was an outburst of song, usually started by Michael.

Michael was in seventh heaven, and the company soon learned why. It was because Laura had promised to marry him as soon as he had staked off their land in the Willamette Valley and built a cabin. Michael didn't know just how he had summoned up enough courage to ask the queen of girls to marry him, but he was glad he did pop the question. She accepted him, in spite of the fact that there was a fine-mannered, educated gentleman, Silas Weeks, waiting for her word. The time of year, by the calendar, was October, with winter just around the bend, but in Michael's heart it was spring. He had plenty of reasons for which to rejoice. A new country, rich land, his own, to be worked and made to blossom and bloom, youth and strength, and the one he loved best in all the world to share it with him. These were the reasons why Michael sang, and the whole Stephen Company, except, no doubt, the disappointed Kentucky schoolmaster, shared his happiness.

❖ ‡ ❖

In the afternoon, Captain Stephen and a group of the company men went up to Fort Vancouver to pay their grateful respects to Dr. John McLoughlin, the superintendent of all the Hudson's Bay Company business in the old Oregon Country. This area covered what is now known as the states of Oregon, Washington, Idaho, and part of western Montana, and western Canada—stretching north all the way to

Alaska. This "country" was inhabited by thousands of Indians and a growing number of new settlers.

The doctor, Canadian by birth, had not been long in gaining the confidence of the Indians. They knew him as a just man, whose word was never broken, and he never failed to punish when punishment was due. So they named him *Hyas Tyee* ("Great Chief"). They also called him *T'kope Latet Chakchak* ("White-headed Eagle") because his hair had turned snowy white before he was forty. Although he was a stern man, the doctor had a heart of gold; a heart that could not let anyone suffer whom he could help. His help to the emigrants in the Far West aroused a storm of protest in far away London. Sir George Simpson, governor-in-chief of the Hudson's Bay Company, believing that Dr. McLoughlin was working against British interests in the Oregon Country, to which Great Britain and the United States then had joint claim, commanded him to stop helping American emigrants with British-owned goods and foodstuffs. The doctor is said to have made this reply: "Gentlemen, if such is your order, I will no longer serve you."

Sir George was far away and could not know how much the pioneers suffered. Dr. McLoughlin saw those in need and could do nothing other than help. He was the kind of man that would not barter away his Christian faith, and heartfelt compassion for others, for the sake of a little more money or earthly power.

A string of forts and trading posts established by McLoughlin at strategic points throughout the country, and a small fleet in the Pacific Ocean, carried on the busy beaver fur trade of the Hudson's Bay Company. Fort Vancouver, in its vantage place on the Columbia, some seven miles above the mouth of the Willamette River, was the chief fort of them all, and the home of Dr. McLoughlin and his family.

Fort Vancouver was a wonderland to the emigrants. It was a striking example of what could be done in this rich country, for the fort was really a complete small town, set in the midst of fertile farms and orchards. Hundreds of men and women, employees of the post, with their children, lived here under the triangular blue flag of the British company. The fort had a school, a hospital, a retail store, a sawmill, a grist mill, barns, stables and granaries, and dozens of homes. A farm of several thousand acres, fenced into beautiful fields, stretched along the river. Fine breeds of livestock thrived on the farm. Lumber was shipped to the Sandwich Islands, and flour to Alaska. There was food in plenty for all those at the post and for thousands more at posts of the company in far-outlying places. When the hungry emigrants began flocking into the

Columbia Valley, Dr. McLoughlin saw to it that there was food for them, too.

To come out of the uncivilized wilderness to this little haven of culture and luxury, was to the covered-wagon travelers like finding the pot of gold at the rainbow's end.

"This fort is not twenty years old, men," exclaimed Captain Stephen. "Of course, there is English wealth behind it, but can't you see what our farms can be like? They say the soil in the Willamette Valley is even richer than this soil, and the timber is just as fine. Look at those granaries filled with grain! Look at those fruit trees and think what the harvest must be! See those milk cows and fat hogs! Did you notice the wool on those sheep?"

The men nodded, as their tired eyes became bright. Here was a golden harvest, reaped by men like themselves from the earth. Who could ask for more? They went back to their camp on the river shore where their tattered wives and children waited with the meager remnants of their household goods. Each man had a shining vision of the home that he would soon build.

The children were playing on the sand with the children of Hudson's Bay employees. Captain Stephen watched them for a while, smiling. It had been a long time since he had seen children smile. Many times in the trials and sorrows of the trail he had reproached himself for having encouraged families with young children to take the dangerous journey. But, today, he was glad. These little ones and their children would gather the harvest in the new country. Less than ten miles down the Columbia was the mouth of the Willamette River. In the valley of that river, their homes awaited them. Only a few weeks more and every man would be staking out his own land. It was not a fool's errand, this long, weary trail to the Oregon Country!

Chapter 27

Journey's End

Springtime in the Willamette Valley is a season of almost supernatural loveliness. Those who know it know beauty that stores itself up in the memory. Green meadows sweeping wide as the eye can see; wild flowers springing in a riot of color; fruit trees laden with promise of the harvest; birds singing as if their hearts were too filled with happiness to hold it all and must burst unless they let the happiness out in song; and, flowing in the midst of this enchantment, the "lovely river softly calling to the sea." The valley of the Willamette is beautiful every spring to all who know it, but to the covered-wagon travelers, come at last to their journey's end, it was an earthly paradise.

The Stephen Company entered the valley just as winter was setting in. The November winds were wailing in the great cedars and firs. They arrived, carrying what remained of their household goods in hired carts. Every soul was tired and threadbare. On French Prairie, so named because it was settled by French-Canadians, the homeless emigrants took refuge in deserted log cabins and in tents. The cabins were poor buildings, but they gave shelter from the wind and rain. Very gratefully, the emigrants moved into the shacks, chinked up the cracks and holes, and took up the difficult business of living through the winter.

The French-Canadians of the settlement had well-stocked farms, and they were kind to the newcomers who faced such problems so bravely. They gave work, whenever they could, to the men and paid them in food and supplies to tide them through the winter. The "Great Tyee" was generous with loans and credits. Without question, he took the word of the emigrants that they would repay the borrowed goods when their farms were bearing. But, between working for other men that winter, toiling early and toiling late, Captain Stephen, Dr. Dean, Michael, Dan, and the others found time to clear their own land, to fence it, to cut timber, to build cabins, and to prepare the soil for the plow.

It was work that went slowly because of the lack of tools. Often the men could have wept, as Hans Sommer did, for the fine tools they had been forced to throw away on the trail; but they accomplished much with what tools they could make and borrow.

Jerry and Jim and all the young boys had their share of work. They whittled thousands of hardwood pegs to be used in building in place of nails. They melted lead and molded bullets. They learned to melt pewter spoons and dishes and mold buttons for their clothing. They cut and carried wood. They helped the men clear the fields; hard work for barefooted boys in the rain. Tanned leather was not to be had, and shoes made from rawhide lost their shape when soaking wet and fell from the feet that wore them.

Even little Myra was put to work braiding strips of cotton rag for wicks to set in saucers of fat to light the cabin. Propped up in the mahogany cradle that had come safely through the hazards of those two thousand miles, Annabelle watched Myra with wide, unblinking eyes, and Myra talked earnestly as she worked. "I'm making light, Annabelle. That's an important thing to be doing, making light."

So they all worked, the little pioneers with the big pioneers, through the long winter. Finally, after what seemed like a lifetime, spring came.

➤ ‡ ◄

One day in April 1845, a long-legged little boy ran up a path that led to a log cabin set in a sunny, cleared place against a background of fir trees. It was a homey-looking cabin, brand new, with a rose vine beginning to creep up beside the door. This vine came from a root that had previously flowered in a far away country. The boy shouted as he ran. "Aunt Beth! Aunt Beth!"

Beth Stephen came to the cabin door to meet the excited child. He held out a handful of small radishes.

"My garden is almost ready to eat!" he cried. "Lettuce an' radishes an' everything—" He stopped to catch his breath.

Beth Stephen took the radishes from the small, warm hand and examined them.

"Almost ready to eat," she mused, "and it's only April."

She looked out over the boy's head at their land, lying smooth and richly-brown and ready for planting. Golden wheat would be rippling there in the sun and wind.

"It's a wonderful country, Jerry," she said. "It's God's own land."

Beth Stephen turned back to her work in the cabin, getting the evening meal ready for her men, who would be coming in from the field soon. Jerry sat in the doorway and watched her. Aunt Beth never rested. He thought that she must work all night, for sometimes, when he woke up in what was certainly the dead of night, he saw her sitting beside the flickering light, sewing, knitting, or carding. She even carded the hair of the despised wolf. Jerry had a vest knitted of "wolf's wool." Sometimes, Uncle Jim laughed and called him "a lamb in wolf's clothing." Aunt Beth was always busy; but she was always happy. She seemed always to have happy things to think about as she served others.

Beth Stephen did have happy things to think about each day. The people of the valley had been so very kind to them. Silas Weeks had opened a school where the children of retired Hudson's Bay men and their Indian wives sat side by side with the little white "Bostons" and learned their lessons.

Laura had no time to teach now. She had a house to keep, for she and Michael had been married early in the year, when Michael and Dan had finished building a cabin. This log cabin had only two rooms, featuring puncheon floors, made of split logs, with tightly-stretched buckskin in place of window glass. In the view of Michael and Laura, however, it was a palace.

Dr. Dean had settled further down the valley on the bank of the Willamette. The French Prairie dwellers were glad to have a doctor among them, and they paid him so well in chickens, hogs, and calves that he soon had a well-stocked farm. The doctor's "rig," drawn by a beautiful snowwhite horse, was a familiar sight on those country roads and lanes. People thought the doctor had given his fine horse an odd name. It was "Wolf's Brother."

Dan and Michael were soon to go back to Fort Walla Walla to drive home the livestock that the company had left there in care of the fort. Devine would go with them, and then, incurable plainsman that he was, he would go on to the States to guide another company of pioneers across the continent.

The ships would be in from Boston in the summer. They would bring to the trading post in the valley at Oregon City material for making clothing, bedding, and, maybe, some tanned leather for shoes. They would also bring needles and pins, dishes and cooking utensils, and such things, dear to the heart of a good housekeeper. Thinking over these things, Beth Stephen sang as she worked.

Jerry, too, was busy thinking big thoughts. A breeze fluttered the white curtain at the window. Aunt Beth was mighty proud of those curtains. A pot of dried-pea soup was steaming on the oak coals in the fire-place, and a row of brown loaves stood cooling on the table. In the short time since they settled, their home was becoming quite comfortable. Someday it would be much finer. Someday they would have a real cook stove, and there would be carpets on the planed oak floors. Uncle Jim said that someday steel rails would be laid across all that country that they had come over in their covered wagons. He said that great iron trains would puff and flash and carry people across the miles in no time at all, bringing, too, everything that they wished for their new home. That would be a miracle, the little boy thought.

He spoke suddenly. "Aunt Beth, I'm going back to Missouri some day."

Beth Stephen turned from the fire to look with amused eyes at the small boy who sat dreaming in the doorway.

"Such a long way, Jerry," she said. "Why would you go? Aren't you happy here?"

"I promised Auntie Kay I'd come back," he answered. "She'll be waiting for me to come."

His aunt turned back to the fire. She didn't speak what was in her mind—poor old Auntie Kay would long be gathered to the far green pastures before her little white lamb returned to the old fold.

A distant shout brought Jerry to his feet. Jim and his father were coming home to supper. Jerry ran to meet them. Beth Stephen went to the door to welcome them home. She noticed that the sky was cloudless

above their heads and that the western sun was like a glory about them.

"Our family is together and safe in a fair land," she thought to herself, then whispered, "God be praised."

their heads and that the western sun was like a glory about them.

"Our family is together and safe in this land," she thought to herself, then whispered, "God be praised."